# KIRBY - SEE ME NOW

TERESA HOUNSLOW

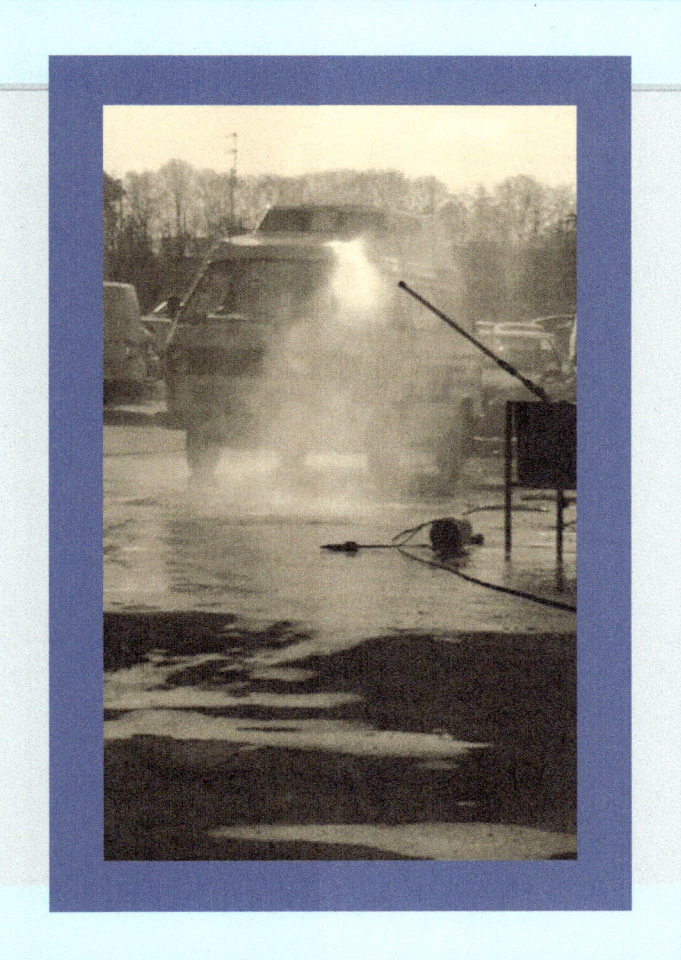

*AuthorHouse™ UK*
*1663 Liberty Drive*
*Bloomington, IN 47403 USA*
*www.authorhouse.co.uk*
*Phone: 0800.197.4150*

*© 2017 Teresa Hounslow. All rights reserved.*

*No part of this book may be reproduced, stored in a retrieval system, or transmitted by any means without the written permission of the author.*

*Published by AuthorHouse 09/20/2017*

*ISBN: 978-1-5246-8282-8 (sc)*
*ISBN: 978-1-5246-8281-1 (e)*

*Print information available on the last page.*

*This book is printed on acid-free paper.*

*Because of the dynamic nature of the Internet, any web addresses or links contained in this book may have changed since publication and may no longer be valid. The views expressed in this work are solely those of the author and do not necessarily reflect the views of the publisher, and the publisher hereby disclaims any responsibility for them.*

authorHOUSE®

## Introduction

If you are the type of person who appreciates the relaxed approach to camping, but loves camper vans and giving them your own personal touch, even if its a unstructured carefree look, then this is a warm easy going alternative and you will love kirby-see me now, also you may not be fully aware of what a learning curve I've taken to get this far. Taking on a DIY project isn't for the faint hearted, and I take my hat off to those who do this for a living. Contradicting my own statement you can achieve much enjoyment from it and the splashes of colour bring a heartwarming welcome. Nevertheless parking up in mellow places where softness and comfort are your surroundings, will bring a sense of peace and relaxation to body and mind.

Well it's been some journey for me and my biggest challenge. I'm far from an expert, as this is my personal journey about doing up my VW T25 on a budget.

I hoped to inspire people to try DIY for a hobby, because it's a great stress reliever/or cause, hmm ???
The point is to encourage you from your comfort zone. If I can attempt DIY so can you. I'm only setting an example that it's ok to fail, and there's a saying that goes...

"Tis a lesson you should heed:
Try, try, try again.
If at first you don't succeed,
Try, try, try again."

Or fail better !

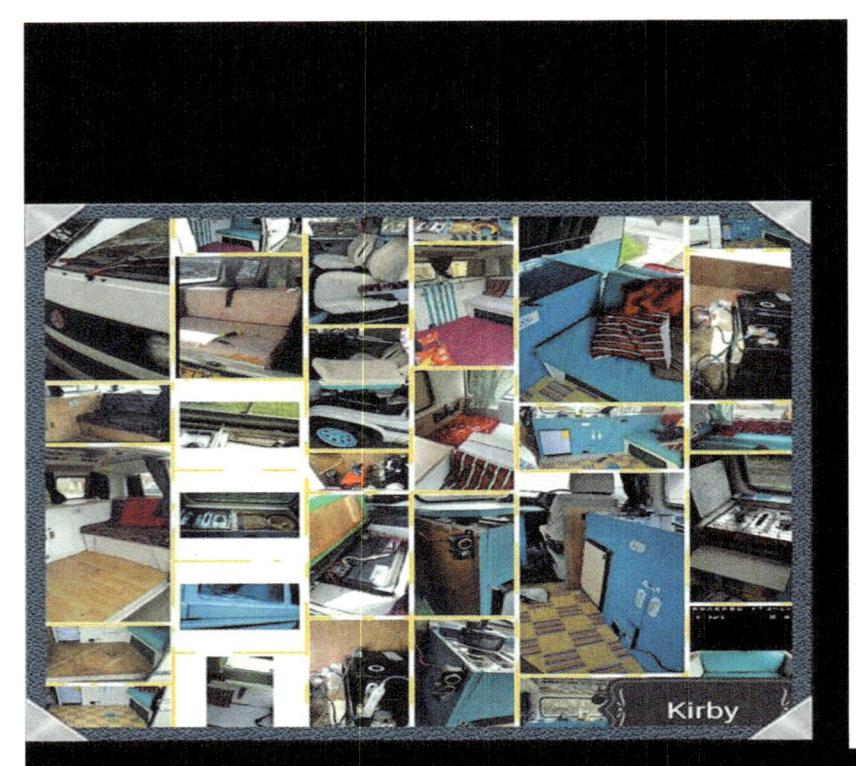

This is just a quick catch up of what was done prior to this book being made. The rock n roll bed is a unique period piece, and a splash of exotic blues transports you to the seashore, combined with reds, whites and yellows.

2

Lets start at the top and work our way down. Here's a before of the ceiling.
I wasn't sure how to tackle this, and kept putting it off. This was done on the lowest possible
budget that could be found, also one's pretty pleased with the results as you will see further along.
I know this has a generous sense of the past but it's not a museum piece and it's time to say goodbye
to this tired old carpet lining and find a more practical design.

Above and left You can see the Original carpeted ceiling, it was very dusty. This was by far the worst job. If you decide to take on a similar project. Even if your taste in decorating and DIY veers to a minimalist, you can always personalize your surroundings with images of family and friends adding a simple throw and some cushions or favourite treasures..

### You need:

Goggles, mask, a sharp Stanley knife and some pliers come in handy to get a good grip of the carpet, as they are glued on pretty well.

Here you can see the roof supports back to bare again, ready for something new. I shall be steering towards some type of washable materials instead of the carpet, which held too must dust for my liking. It may not be glamorous but it shall be truly personal and distinctive. Just above the roof supports, this was a utilitarian ingenious storage shelf, but it's time to find something more aesthetically pleasing.

Here's a quick view of the roof inside before I rip it all out.
Those insulation squares were another mistake as they added too much weight. One things for sure I've certainly given some of my friends great amusement who like to kindly tease me about my terrible DIY. To which I agree and luckily I have a sense of humor, plus I find great pleasure from just enjoying adding my own personal touches. Besides it's a great stress buster.

So I started ripping things out, will it all come together again, at this point I'm still thinking what have I done, please let it be ok. Organised chaos springs to mind, but this battered old carpet and shelving is going.

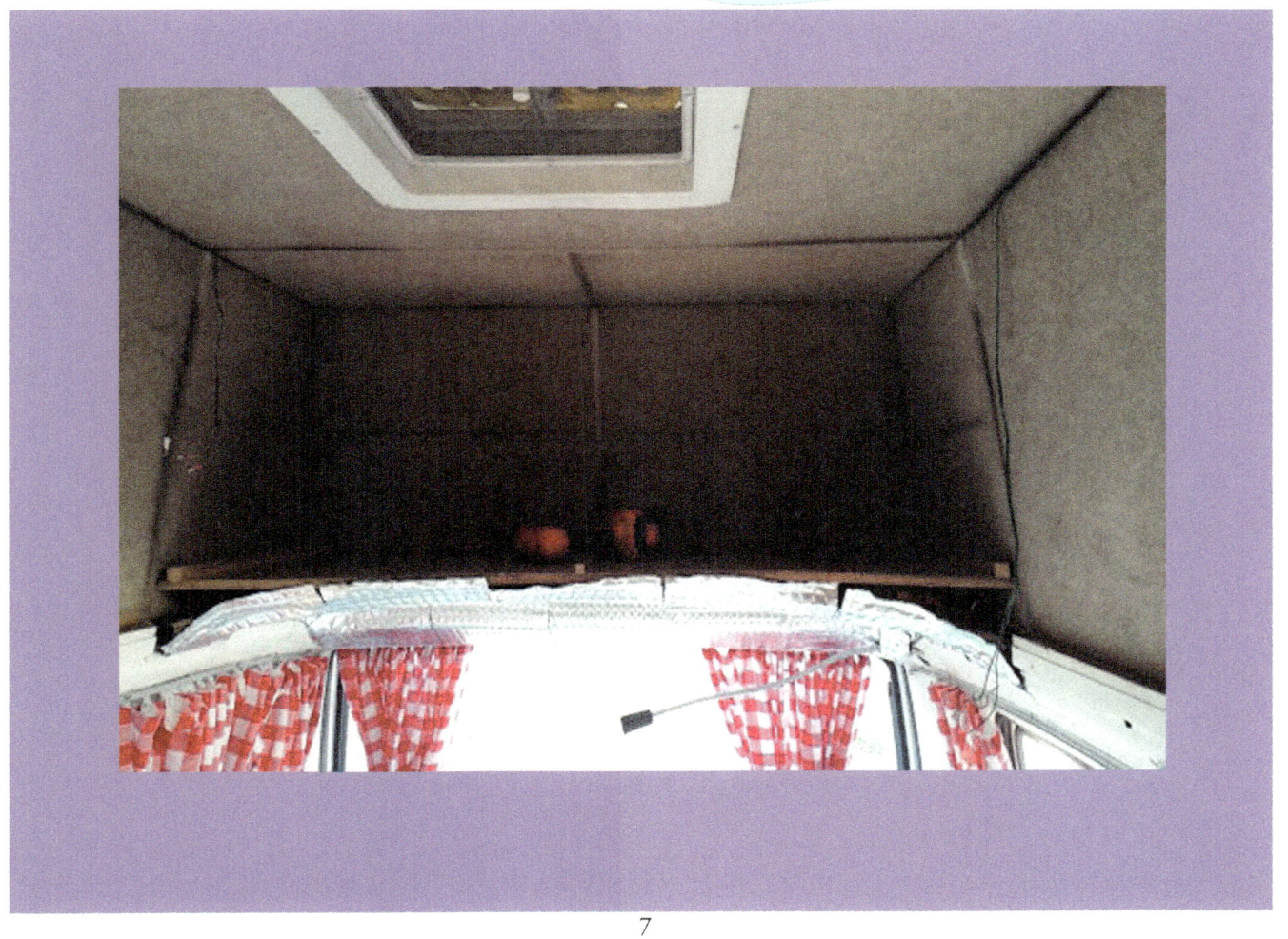

So at this point I was attempting to get away with spending nothing, as I have paint laying around in the garage. Nope, that didn't work, the boards were too rough even after sanding first they had, had it. Don't panic, mismatched things help to create a easy going atmosphere so I hear.

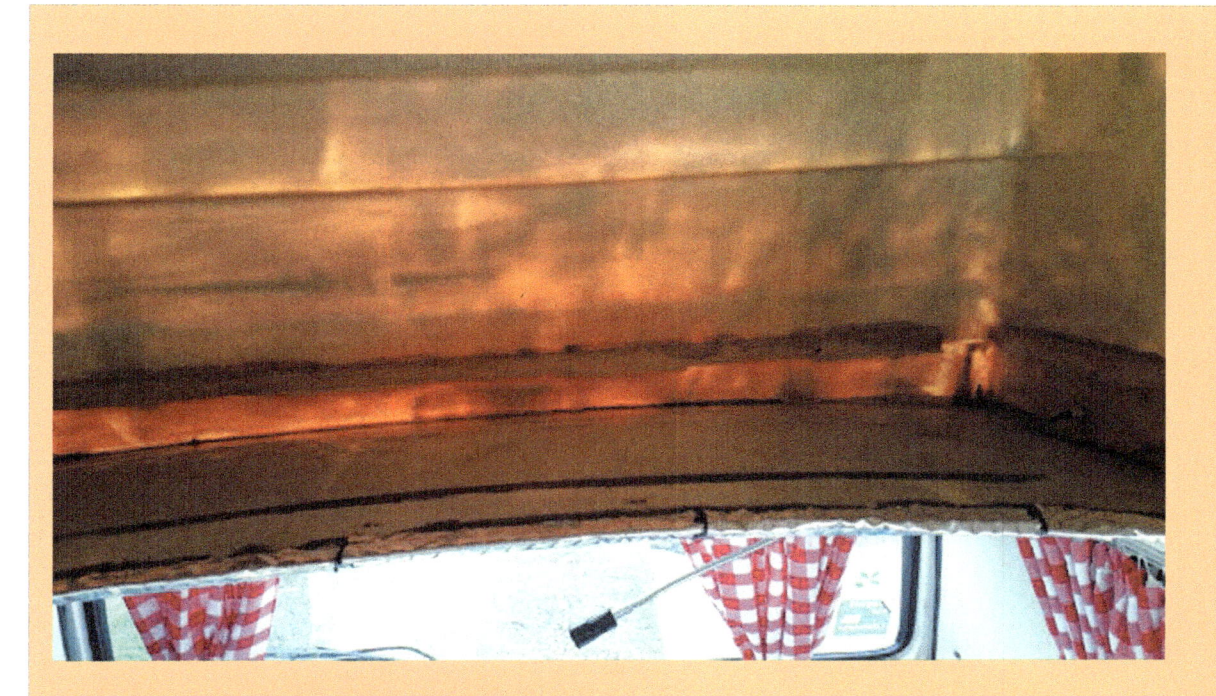

So I'm finally back to the bare shell, its pretty scary when you get to this
basic canvas, it's hard to visualize where I'm going next with it.
All I know at this point is it cant get any worse.
If you take on a project like this remember it doesn't have to be costly.   When it comes to
a relaxed camper fix up, there is more scope for your imagination

I found this fabulous material It was £3.25 per sq m.
Think generously they say, I say think generously towards your own pocket and buy the cheapest nicest one and save the rest, to achieve a Cossetted feeling.

**You will need:**
1. Glue gun or tube glue.
2. Sharp craft knife.
3. Self adhesive insulation

Finally the insulation is up, it had none in when I removed the panels, which explains why it was so cold when we went camping. This "self adhesive" roll of van* insulation was so much easier to apply than having to get out the duct tape. It's very important to use the correct materials because glues give off nasty toxins if they heat up, as vans get very hot inside in summer.
I would like to achieve a welcoming focal point but maybe I should stick to adding the patchwork quilts and pillows, but then that can come later as I have to get this messy part finished before I can sit and enjoy the cosy van.

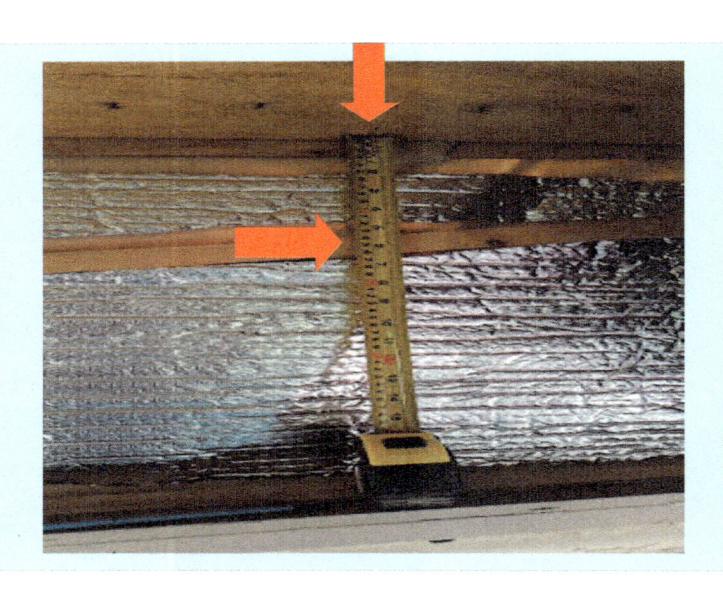

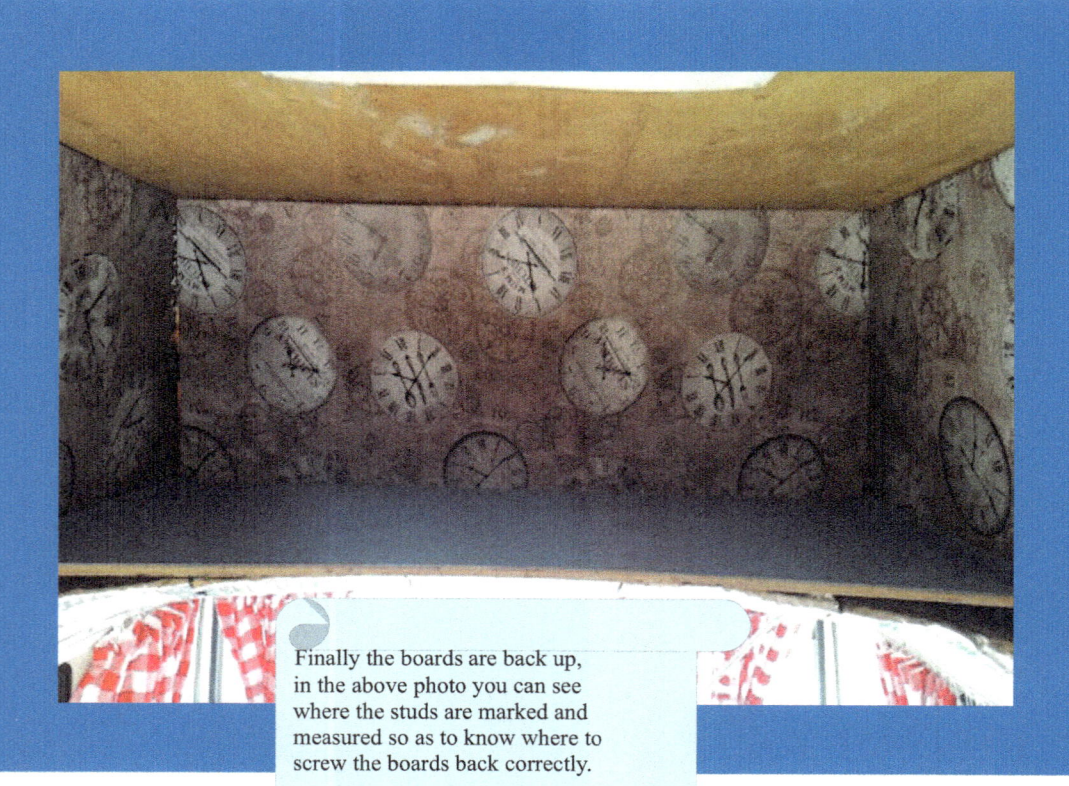

Finally the boards are back up, in the above photo you can see where the studs are marked and measured so as to know where to screw the boards back correctly.

**Tip:**
Do as I say
Not as I do..
(Not my quote, but a good one nevertheless.)

I must mention that I used a washable material, hoping it will be making light work of the routine when it comes to maintaining and cleaning the van in future. I know its not to everyones comfort but to my needs, its perfect as I like to be able to wash it down and freshen it up. These old vans hold a lot of dust going by what I ripped out, I don't ever want be that dusty again. But again to justify it was within a amazing budget. (much cheaper than carpet) There was a lot of other materials that were lovely and colourful with gorgeous patterns, but I had a budget and determined to stick within it, so I decided on the best within that price range.

The Fablon is a faux leather effect in tan.
I found gently pressing in the middle and working the air out toward the edges the best method to apply.

Every body loves a before and after.. especially a happy ever after. I hope this is mine.

I needed help as this is what I call fabulous "fablon," It's self adhesive and very reasonable to purchase. Remember when you lay back in the evening this will be one of your main focus points and makes a easier going atmosphere, then more inclined to be relaxed.

**Here's a tip:**
You get more for your money If you buy the larger rolls. This is a lot easier to apply if there are two of you, unless you have very long arms..." just for ceilings" you may need the extra hands, doing worktops for example would obviously be easy enough to do single handed.

Well here's a hint of what my next plan is. Chunky pine alongside Plywood. I know I'm supposed to buy Marine ply wood, but I'm on a budget and its more expensive. (I shall seal it with varnish). I have to say long term buy the best, but I change my mind a lot and next year it will be changed again no doubt. This could just be my contemporary piece of art work.

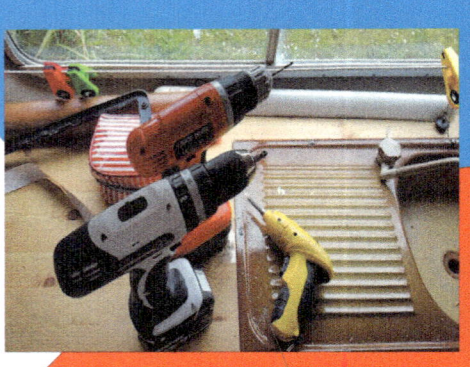

**Tip:** I found it faster to use multi tools rather than keep changing over the bits.

The benefits of buying sheet wood, is they will cut it free for you if you go in ready with your measurements.
This was a blessing.
This is 12mm ply.

**Long term tip:**

I must repeat go for the marine ply.

Ok. Maybe I over compensated here with the slats. I just knew my children would be climbing up at The same time, so there you go a good excuse to make it really strong. In actual fact The wood isn't very heavy. Oh* and yes it's a bunk bed I designed myself... one proud momma. I must add, the gaps between the wood are there to let the mattress breath. I may add a few 2" round holes in the ply "randomly" for more air circulation later on. Now I have the foundation all I need to do now is create a super soft bed with blankets and pillows and some cosy personal toys for the children to comfort them, to bring a homely feeling along to our trips.

Looking more like a bed. I was kindly donated these blue roll out camping mattresses. We may throw on A duvet to make it extra soft, but they are ideal as there is very limited space. Perfect for someone very slim or a child. I can't even tell how long I was stuck up there trying to screw those boards down. On a lighter note this experience was highly amusing  Perhaps this could inspire someone to build there own bunk in their own van. I would be very flattered if that was the case, because most of my ideas fail (chuckle).

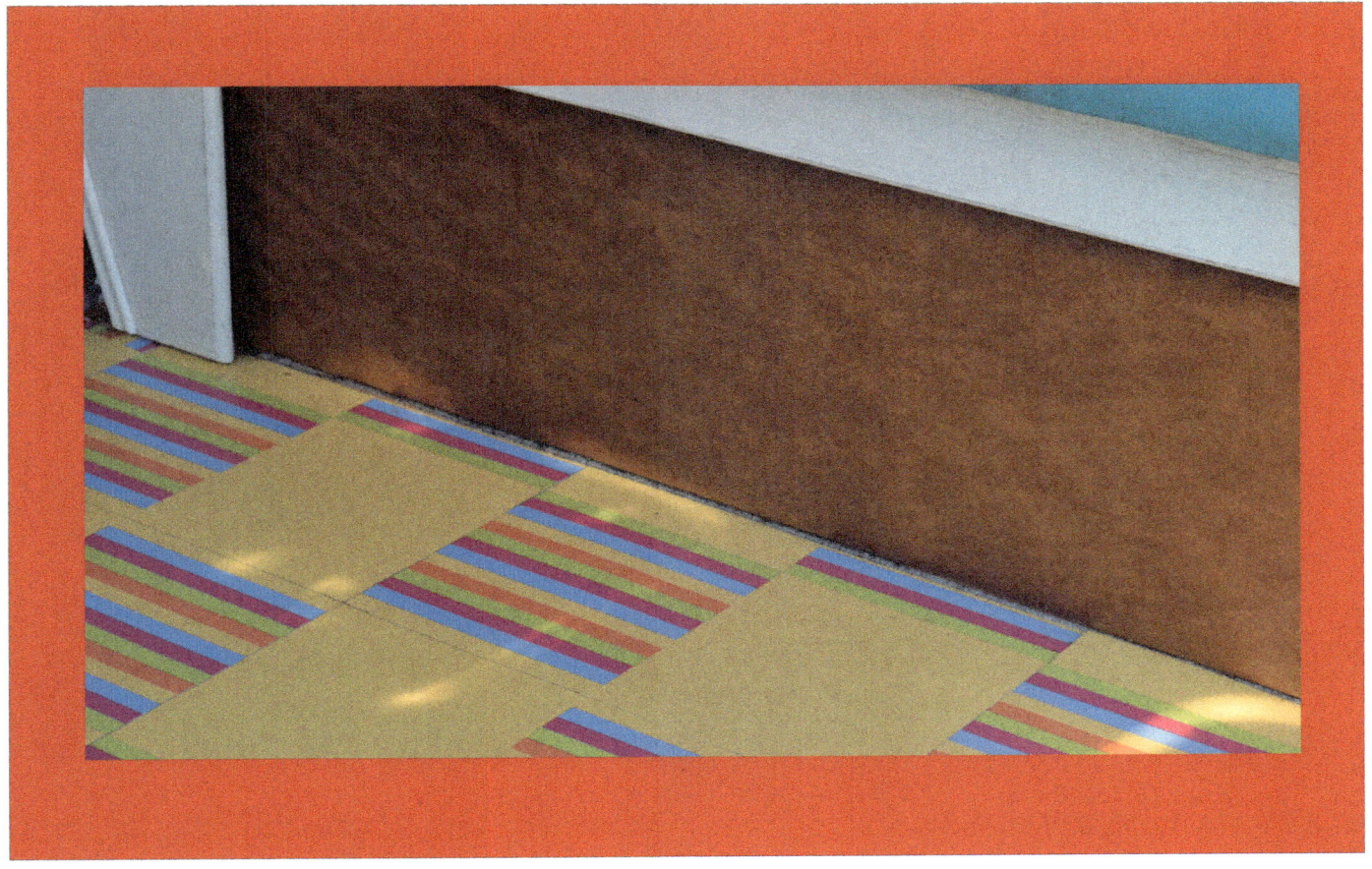

Before and after the Fablon. I could quite happily cover my whole house in this amazing Product.
I decided to lay fablon over the top of the felt because it give it a padding and soft to the touch feel and looks more Realistic. This vivacious blue contrasts nicely with the brown.

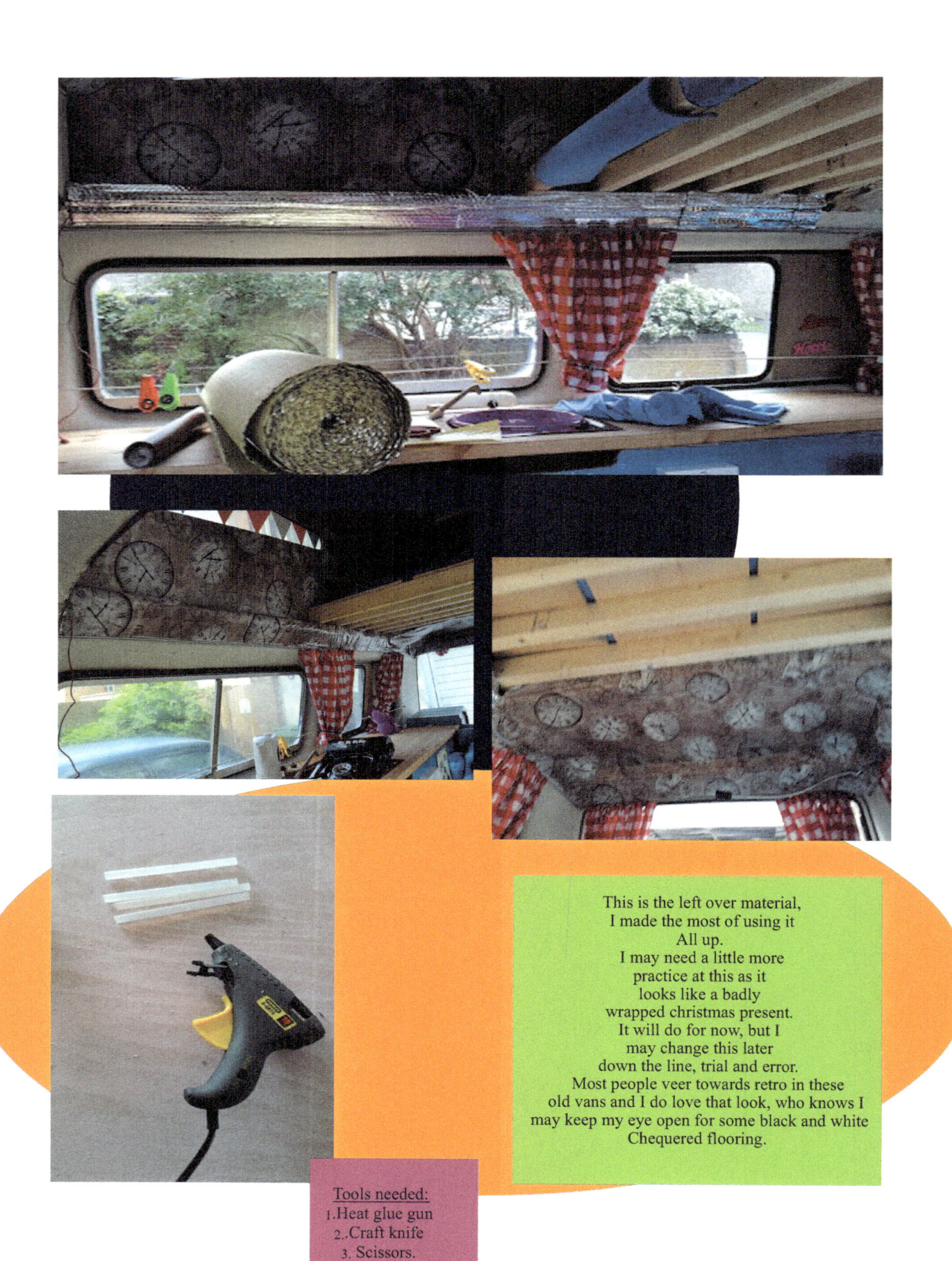

This is the left over material,
I made the most of using it
All up.
I may need a little more
practice at this as it
looks like a badly
wrapped christmas present.
It will do for now, but I
may change this later
down the line, trial and error.
Most people veer towards retro in these
old vans and I do love that look, who knows I
may keep my eye open for some black and white
Chequered flooring.

Tools needed:
1. Heat glue gun
2. Craft knife
3. Scissors.

Not in order of how the jobs panned out, but here is that material again making its way onto the panels. There wasn't a lot of insulation so that has been done also before panel replacement. The brownish clock material again brings out the bold blue on the bed.

This rear panel was attached behind
The unit so the only way around it was to just cover it this way. The wood was very rough. Again fablon and insulation make a great team. There was strong suggestions that I rip out the lot and start again, but to my amusement I like now tormenting those persons, with my humorous attempts Of DIY. I must add stating the difference in cost brings a genuine smile.

Recovery of the boot door panel in Fablon and insulation applied.
I've left the material under the Fablon because I wanted a soft headboard. It also gives a delicate counterpoint to the blue bed.

Again the process of redoing all the panels I did last year, the material is what I have purchased at a generously low cost, and this way I can achieve a new look. Not to forget to mention that the insulation really needed doing to make our camping trips more comfortable.

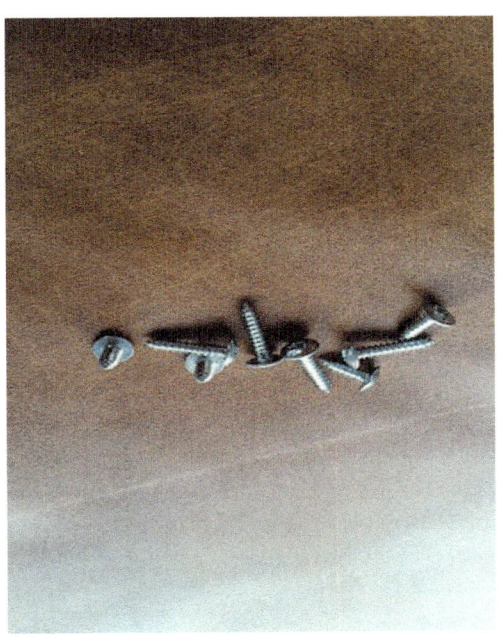

All of the panel screws had gone rusty so have now been replaced with newer wider headed ones.

You may notice the door cards are damaged on the corners. I do intend later down the line to replace with a thin marine ply instead. I have to work that into the budget when I can afford it. It's taken me well over a year to slowly replace things but it's getting there slowly, it's quite therapeutic too. This brown is much nicer than the bright blue as it brings a warmer tone to the décor.

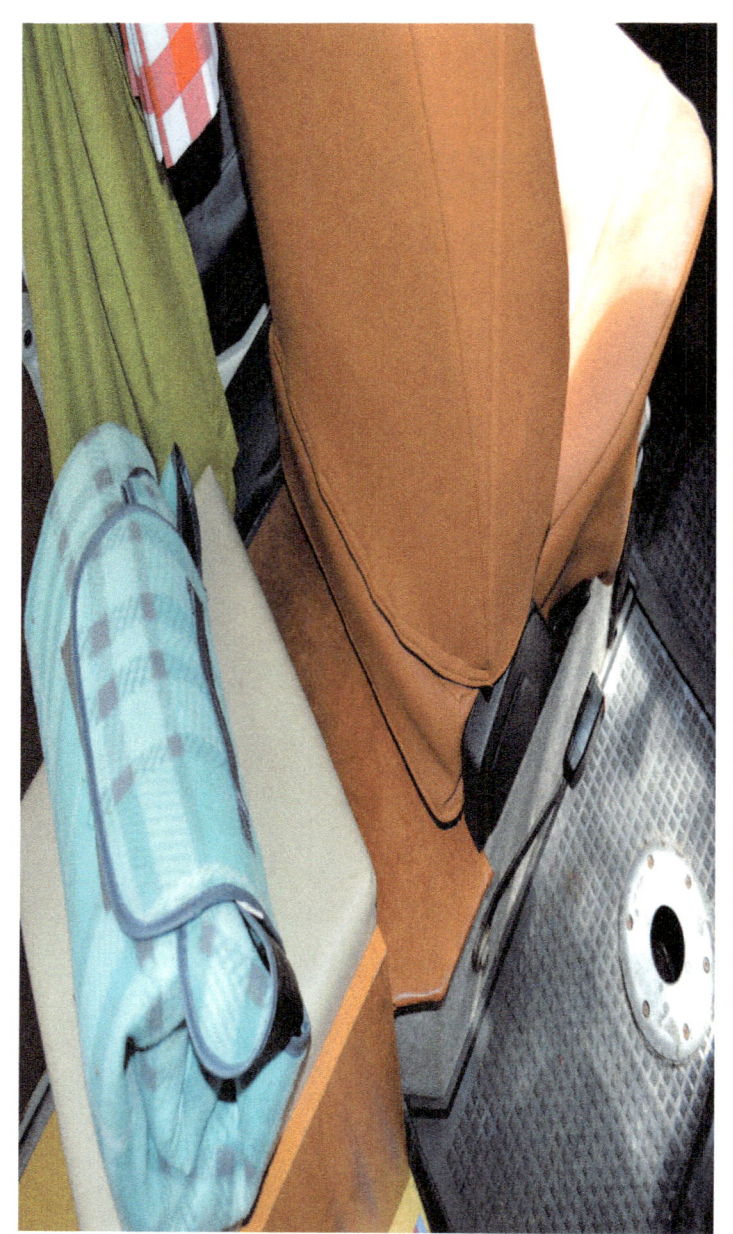

These little lids that sit nicely over the battery and storage box behind the front seats, have had a new lease of life with this Fablon. I am yet to do the sides, but not decided if I want to go buying more materials just yet because I might just go back to the bare metal and paint it.

Last year I covered these
in an old pillowcase.
This year I've discovered a
wonderful thing
called chalk paint.
I haven't added much attention
to detail on these due to
the fact that I need to stay
In budget even if it means sacrificing
some other pieces of furniture
to achieve this useful extra
needed mirror.

Chalk painted, then sealed with clear wax.
**Tip:** make your own Chalky type paint "1 part" plaster of paris "2 parts" water based Paint..

I like the pink?

Made from a
Pot handle!

I made a mess
With the glue.
On the up side it
Hasn't fell off yet..

Apparently I should be
Calling this my mistake
Page, but I find them very
Amusing.
I was just making a point
that I could replace parts
for free. When I looked at
how much the handle was
to buy, I decided to try to
Fix it myself. In fact all
that was broken
was it had snapped off shorter.
I thought well
there must be another solution to this.
So there you go a pot handle is still
a handle after all.

Last year you may of already seen that I just copped out from making covers and threw over some shop ones only just customising them a little..
Well I'm doing the same this year but these were bought to order for the VW vans.
Except they are a nicer colour.
But bare with me they look Great!

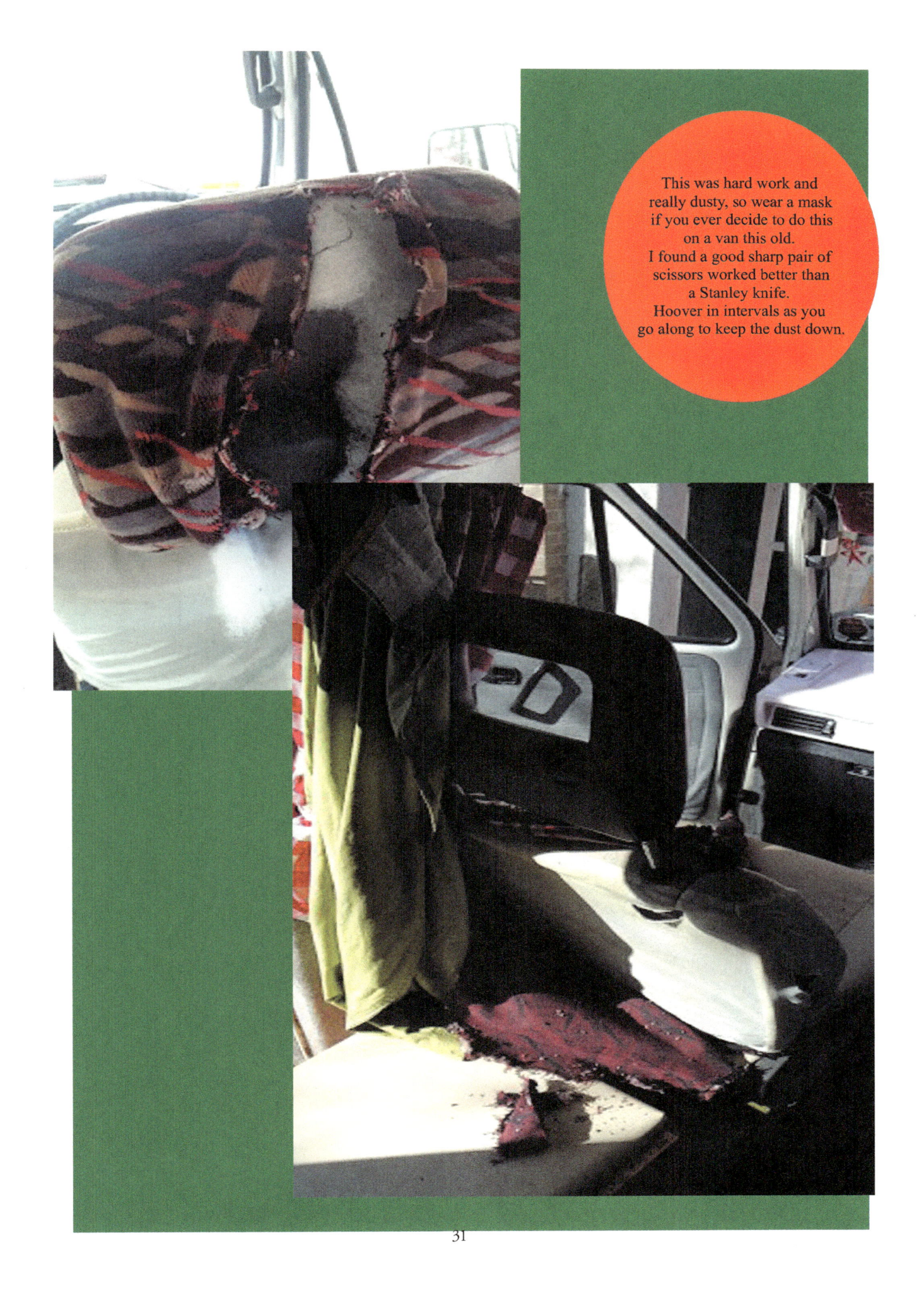

This was hard work and really dusty, so wear a mask if you ever decide to do this on a van this old.
I found a good sharp pair of scissors worked better than a Stanley knife.
Hoover in intervals as you go along to keep the dust down.

Well I'm very impressed. Before and after.
My arm rests belonged to a ford transit and so did
my head rests. I removed the arm rests, prefer them
without. But this was still a big saving compared
to taking the seats into a company for recovery. It finally
feels like it's starting to come together at this point.

I couldn't wait to let you see this, of course I take my pictures mid work, so its not very tidy but this is me, I get very impatient and want it done. I didn't think I was capable, but I was showed how, and now I know how easy it is. Setting myself an example this time from my own comfort Zone.
Who knows you might even find the courage to tackle that DIY you been putting off.

Silicone: don't forget this to go around the sink and taps. After all that hard work you don't want any plumbing leaks.

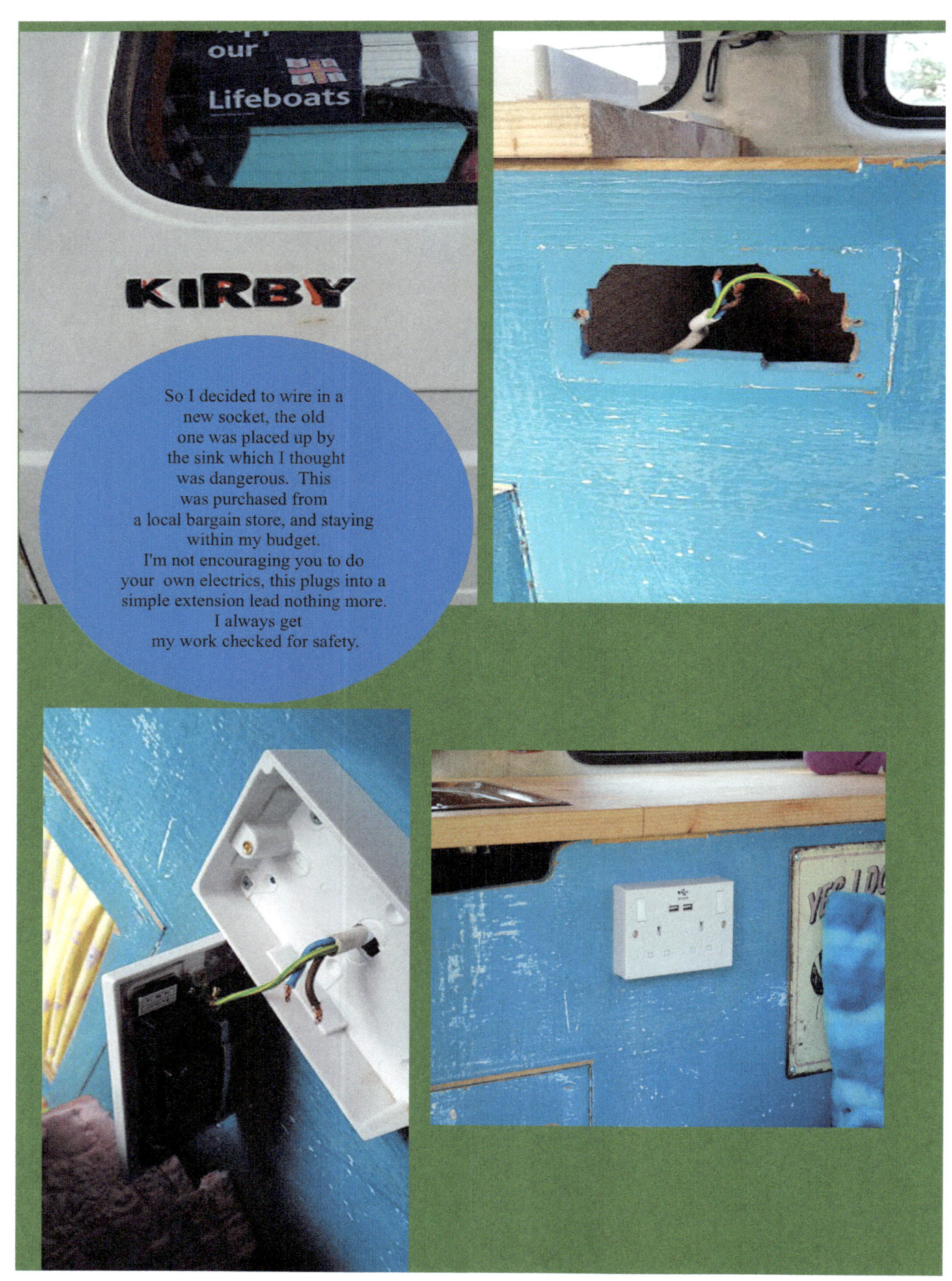

So I decided to wire in a new socket, the old one was placed up by the sink which I thought was dangerous. This was purchased from a local bargain store, and staying within my budget. I'm not encouraging you to do your own electrics, this plugs into a simple extension lead nothing more. I always get my work checked for safety.

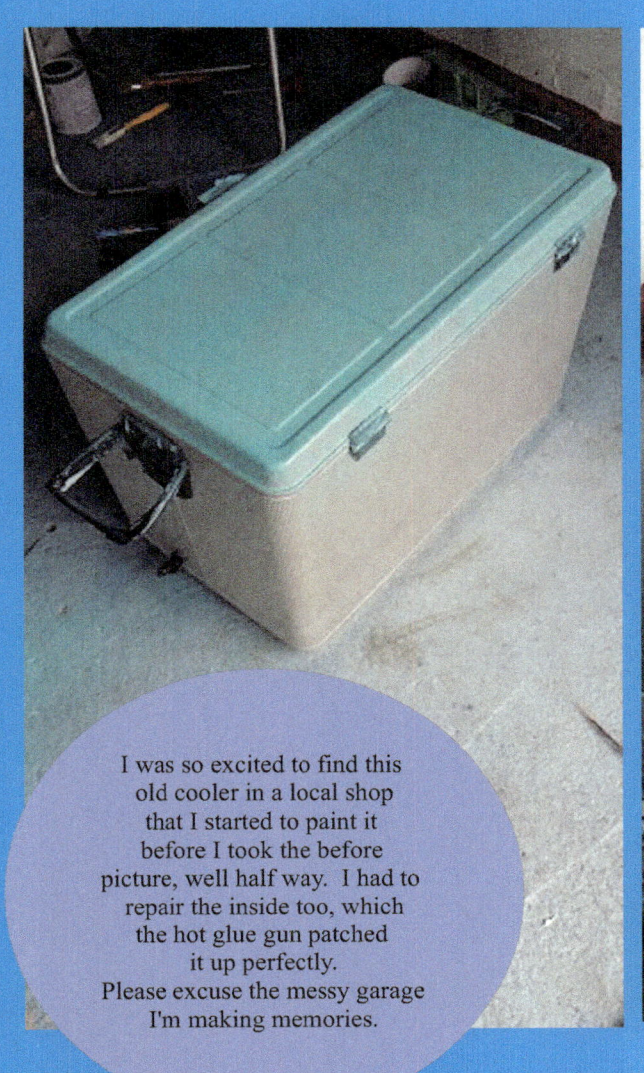

I was so excited to find this old cooler in a local shop that I started to paint it before I took the before picture, well half way. I had to repair the inside too, which the hot glue gun patched it up perfectly.
Please excuse the messy garage I'm making memories.

I wanted a YETI but I promised to do this on a budget.

This needs a new door card really but I'm hoping to find an alternative way around just replacing the rotten part in the bottom corner. Not so much cost, as hard board is fairly cheap, but its more the fact that I have to take all the handles off... hmm? I might save this job until last. You see I also have my reserves but then once I try to tackle them it's not so bad, especially If you take photos as you go, so you know how to put It back together.

Started with the primer. I know I know, in my defence I'm a laid back DIYer, try not to judge me too harshly with my not so great skills. I'm doing this for my own entertainment and if it entertains you also, then I'm happy I bought joy to your time, especially if you have a camper.

Masking is not one
Of my
greatest talents.

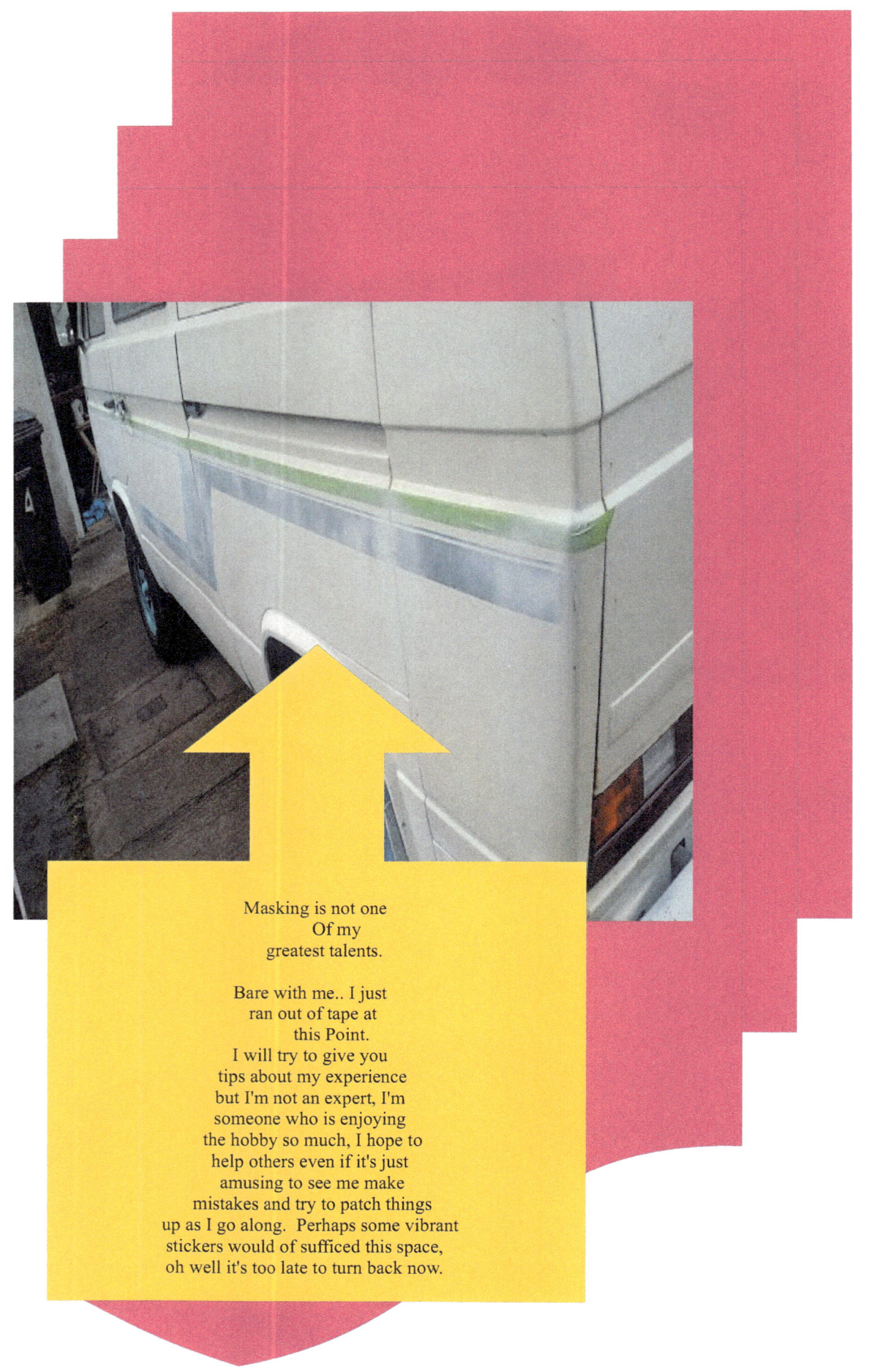

Bare with me.. I just
ran out of tape at
this Point.
I will try to give you
tips about my experience
but I'm not an expert, I'm
someone who is enjoying
the hobby so much, I hope to
help others even if it's just
amusing to see me make
mistakes and try to patch things
up as I go along. Perhaps some vibrant
stickers would of sufficed this space,
oh well it's too late to turn back now.

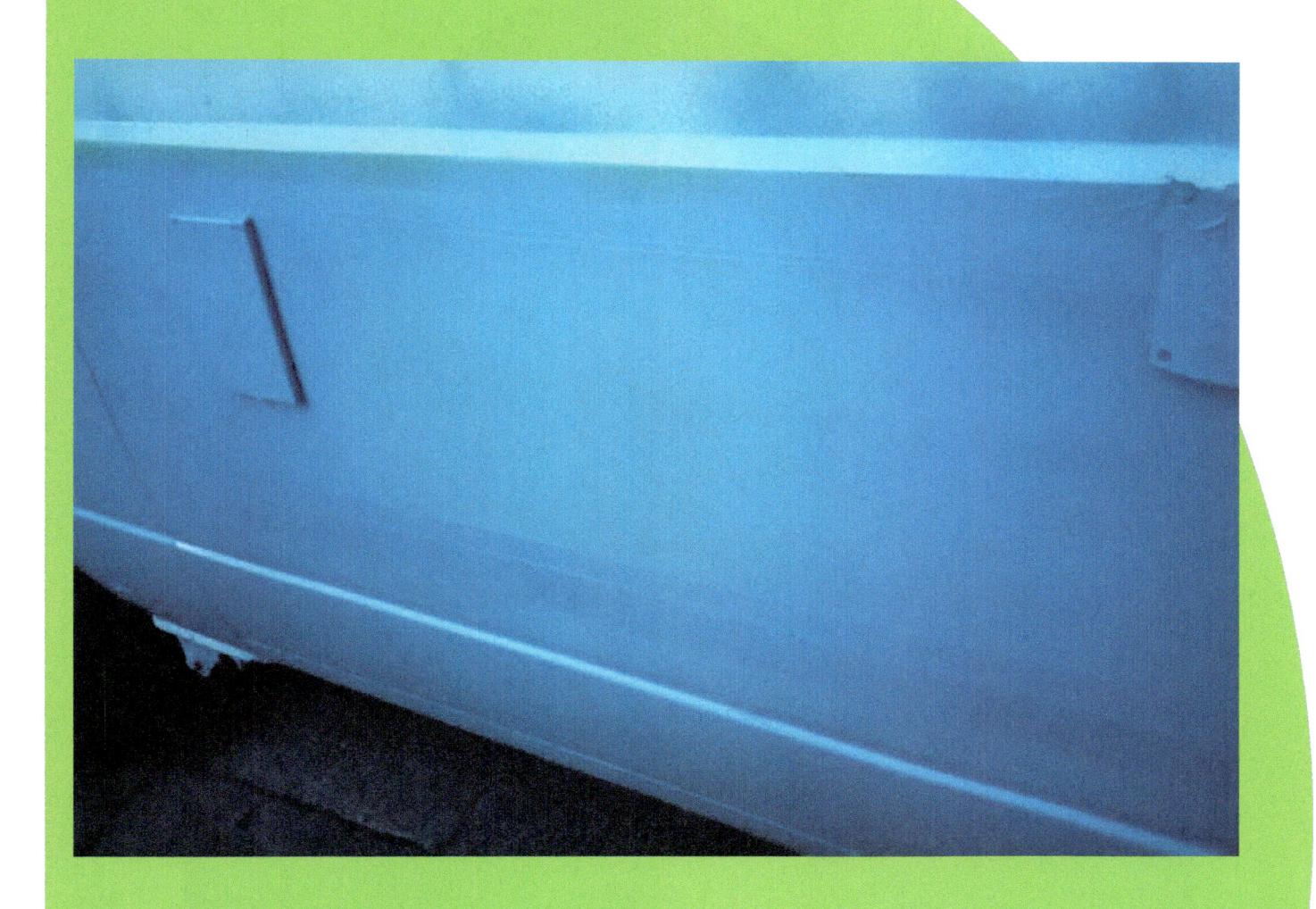

**Tips:**
1. Choose your location wisely, preferably not under a tree, And check the weather will be fine for a couple days.

2. Mask up well "learn from my mistake, just see my wheels!".
3. Prepare the surface. Sand, prime, & treat any rust.

4. When applying do lots of light coats, rather than one heavy one, as the paint will run.

5. Give plenty of drying time before using it to protect it.

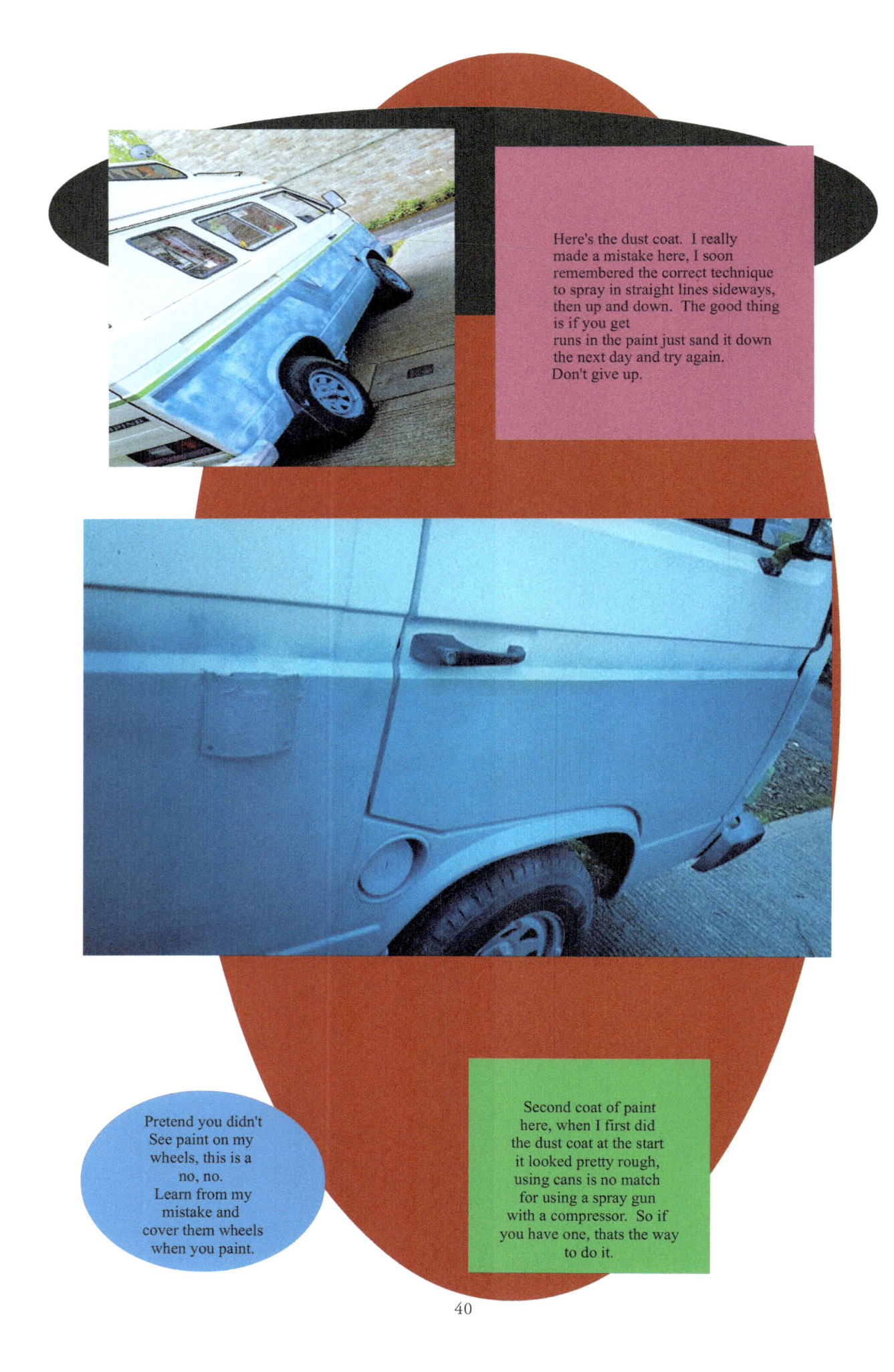

Here's the dust coat. I really made a mistake here, I soon remembered the correct technique to spray in straight lines sideways, then up and down. The good thing is if you get runs in the paint just sand it down the next day and try again. Don't give up.

Pretend you didn't See paint on my wheels, this is a no, no. Learn from my mistake and cover them wheels when you paint.

Second coat of paint here, when I first did the dust coat at the start it looked pretty rough, using cans is no match for using a spray gun with a compressor. So if you have one, thats the way to do it.

I'm not decided yet where I want this line to be...

("Bit late now it's there Woman.. ! ")

I'm quite liking the white at the top actually, I may just clean it up and neaten that line.

I kid you not, but every single time
I hold a can of paint in my hand and
attempt to spray this van, the rain
comes down within 10 mins.
I feel like the unluckiest person,
as I would have had it finished ages ago
if the weather would give me a break.

My poor attempt at
keeping the rain off
My still wet paint.

If only I had a gazebo, and
that big tree would
Stop dripping all over the
Van...
If only..
Hey keep reminding yourself
you saved £900 on a paint job.

Tip:

Never give up !

Kirby needs more coats but not the wheels..( chuckle).. You need to keep a sense of humour if your going to take on a project like this, because it will push you in every direction but eventually you will reach your goal..

Just some before's of the rust.

Is it me, or does it look like someone's inside the van ?

Someone please remind me why I started this project.. I'm having a overwhelmed day. I may stick to just painting up my children's furniture when this is finished...
Will it ever be finished?

There is only so much rust one can stand to look at.

Rust is starting to haunt me.

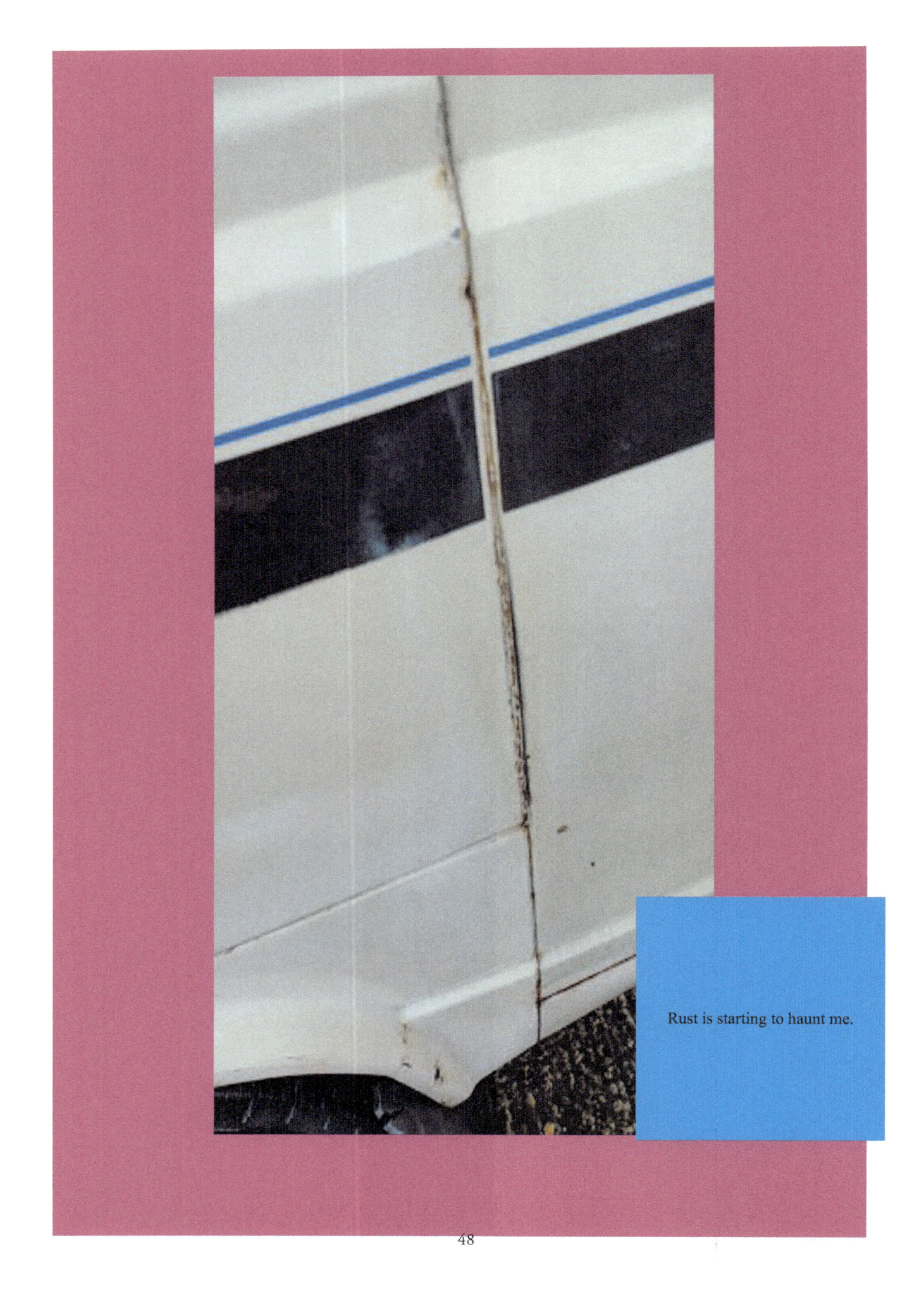

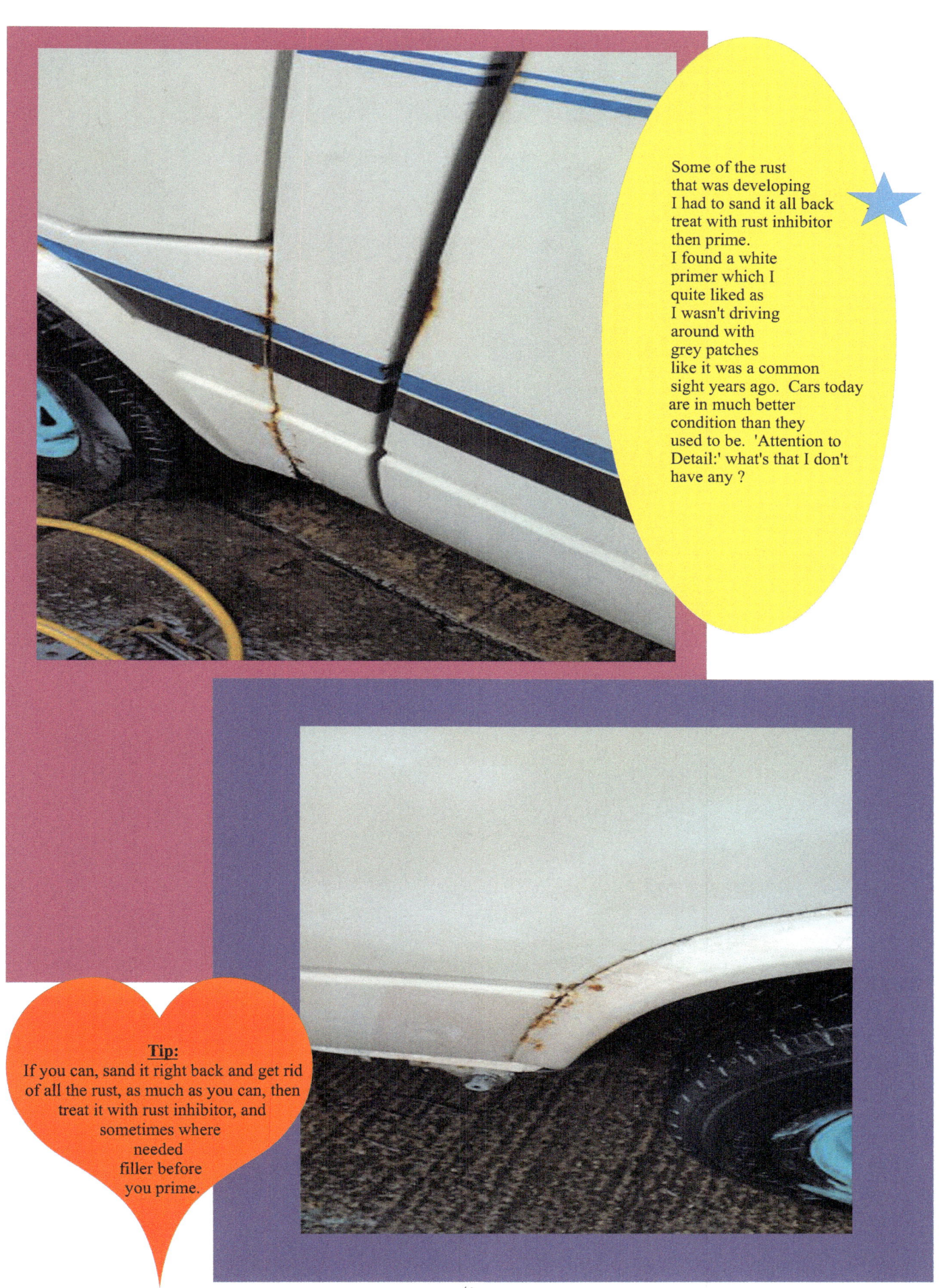

Some of the rust that was developing I had to sand it all back treat with rust inhibitor then prime.
I found a white primer which I quite liked as I wasn't driving around with grey patches like it was a common sight years ago. Cars today are in much better condition than they used to be. 'Attention to Detail:' what's that I don't have any ?

**Tip:**
If you can, sand it right back and get rid of all the rust, as much as you can, then treat it with rust inhibitor, and sometimes where needed filler before you prime.

I placed a few of these under the
lid of the new worktop
to stop it sliding around when the vans
on the go, because I still need to lift it up
to access the water and gas bottles.

I'm working on this, something will
pop into my head later on and I'm sure it will
be a one off idea, and will amuse people.

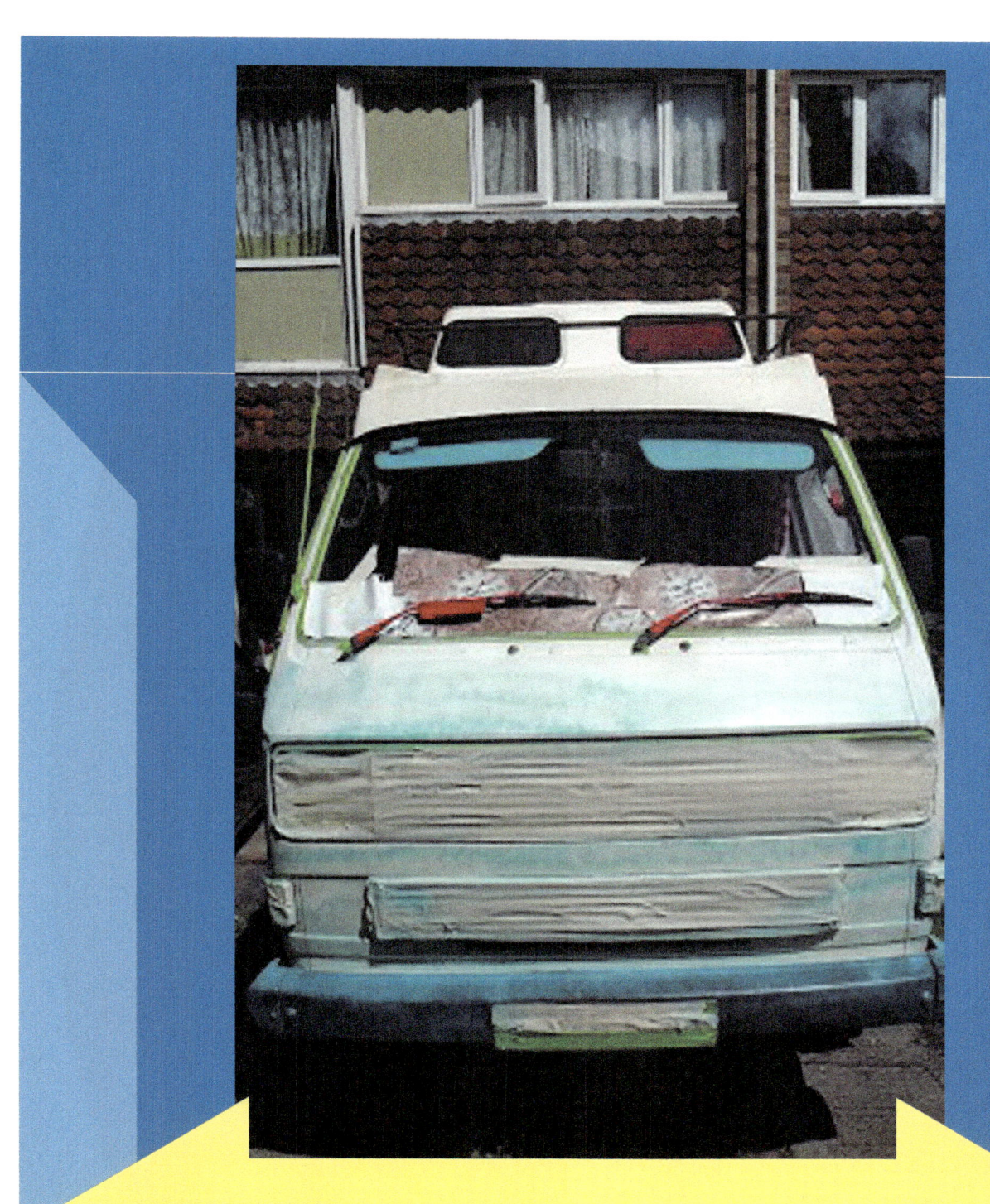

I'm not sure if I'm coming or going at this point, it's "exhausting" … pardon the pun!

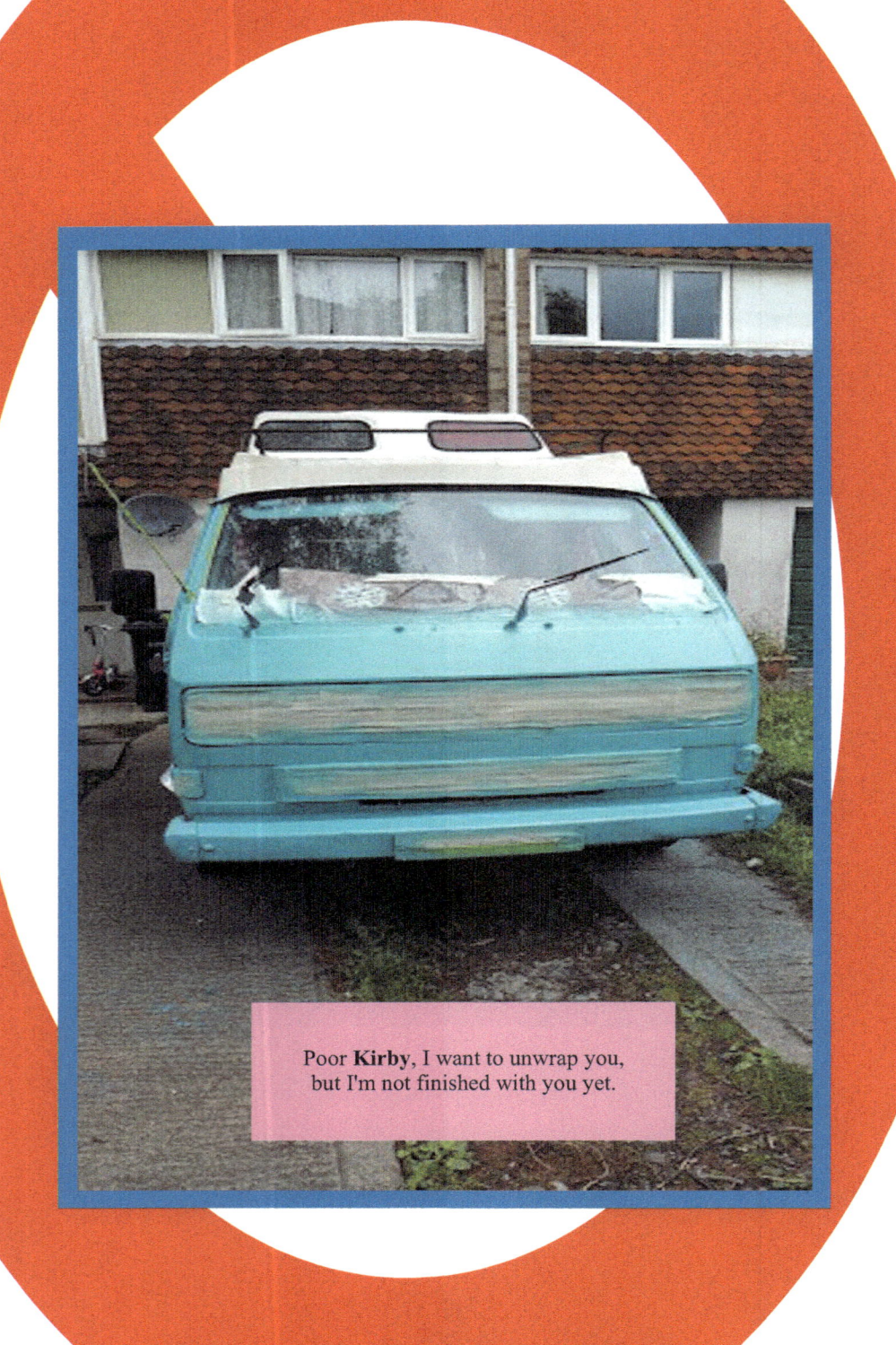

Poor **Kirby**, I want to unwrap you, but I'm not finished with you yet.

Love this colour.

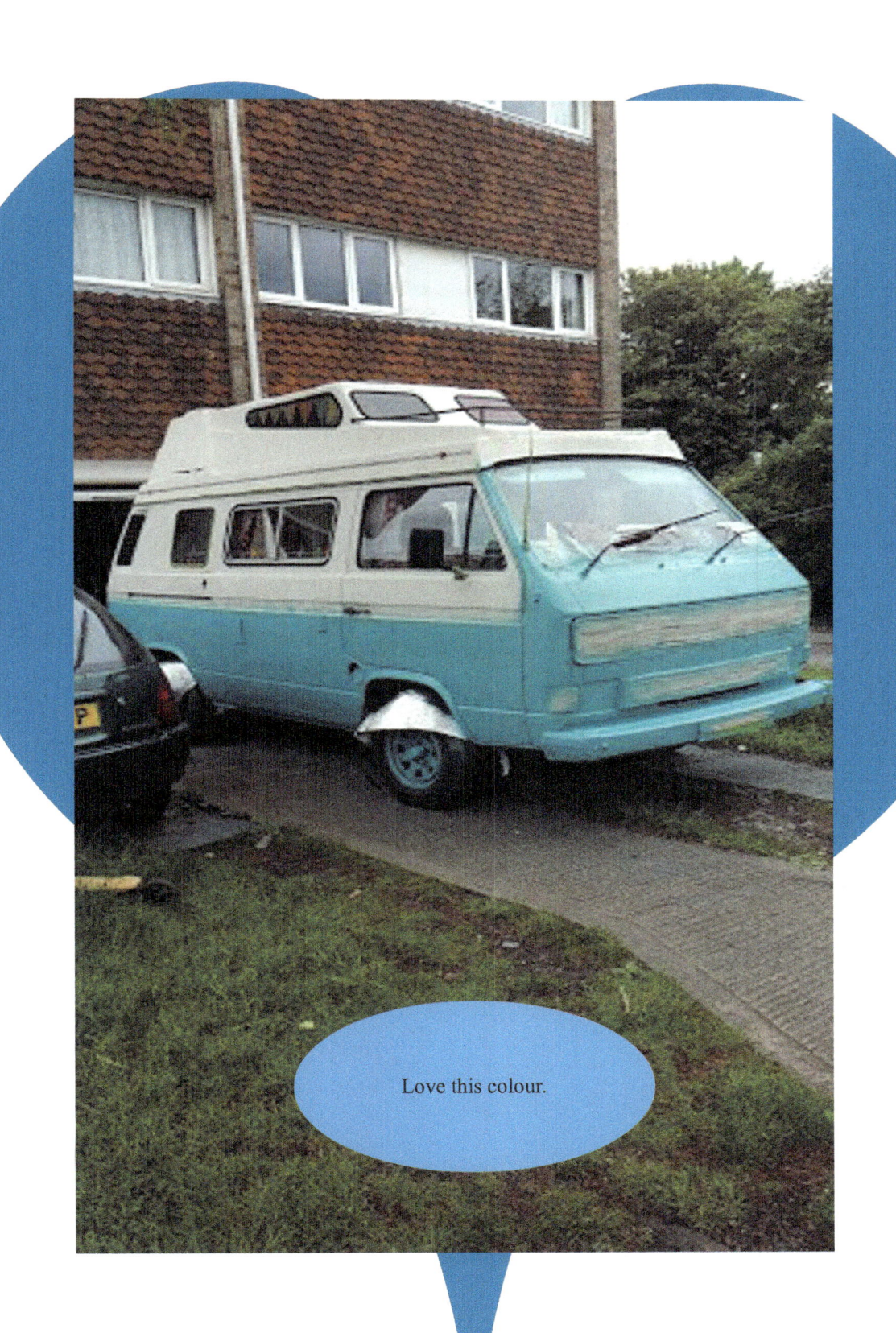

**Tip :**
Being casually relaxed about these projects, ensures a sense of inner peace, and allows for a more stress free and more productive outcome.

I'm very close to the finish but with the weather and the limited time I get to fit it in. I'm thinking here I have to mask up all that bottom half to spray the upper half. I should of started From the top.

(sigh). The silver birch tree isn't giving me a break from constantly dripping sap all over the wet paint, I won't let it stop me.

Here I've decided to do something a little different with the joining line, so I'm hoping it turns out ok..

I tend to stay open minded with my designs and go with the flow, see how it turns out attitude. This way I won't be disappointed if I don't achieve what I set out to do. So at this point I'm considering doing a misty joint line.

Quite pleased with how its' panning out so far.

Still needs more coats but Kirby is beginning
to come together at last.
at this stage I have no idea how I will
tackle the next step of the top half..
So far I've had one can of paint explode all
over me and drip big dollops
on the van, so I had to sand them bits back.
A simple painting design is often the
most effective and is the easiest to achieve.

**You need** : Masking tape and copious amounts of it.
Lots of sanding back first, my arm aches!
Well everyone hated my blue wheels when I
First painted them, but now they blend in, I knew
there was method to my madness.  Don't underestimate
the number of tins of paint you will need.  This still needs
a few more coats.  I will give it a while to harden and t cut
at a later date to smoothen the finish, and lacquer.

I removed the cooker then replaced it with a portable one.

I can now cook outside in the Sunshine.
This also frees up my worktop space with It's clean tidy new design. aesthetically pleasing to the eye.

**Tips:**

1. Don't let anyone tell you that you can't do something because you are not good enough.
Does it really matter If your paint runs? It's not the end of the world if someone starts being negative towards your ideas. Stop worrying about what other people think and go for your dreams.
2. Tell yourself," I am capable of overcoming obstacles in my life."

This has been an amazing experience which I've enjoyed to the full extent. I will be honest it's not all easy there is ups and downs great days, and really hard days, even weeks where you get nothing done at all. Depending on how hectic life gets I try to fit a little DIY into my spare time because you should never give up dreaming to improve your life, no matter how tough things get ...keep moving forward!

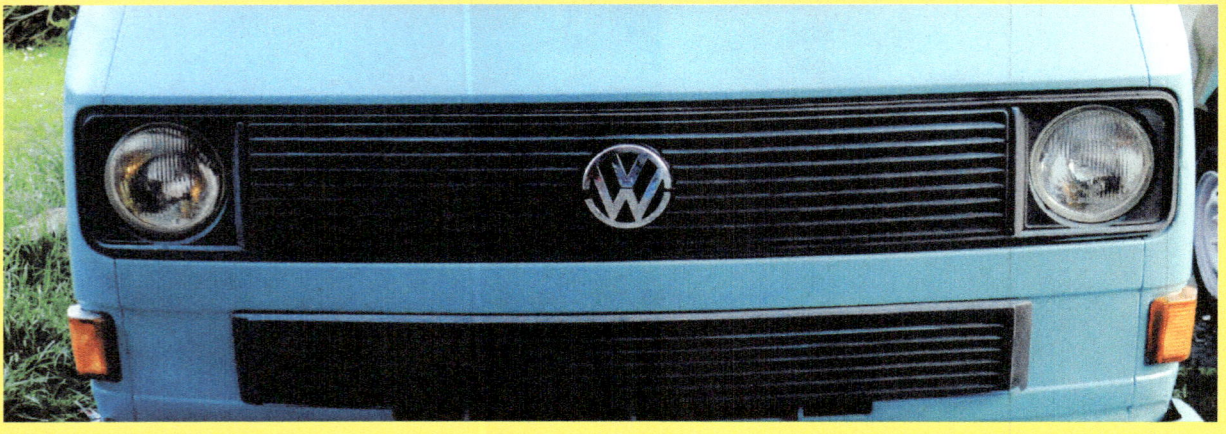

I left the middle section misty, because well it's different and I haven't seen one like this before. I still need to clean up to the top half not quite done Yet.
I would like to take this opportunity to Thank you for reading my book, I sincerely hope you found as much amusement seeing my mistakes as much as I enjoy attempting doing DIY. I really do sit back with a sense of humour and I'm fully aware of mishaps I make, but I wouldn't have It any other way.

Gallery

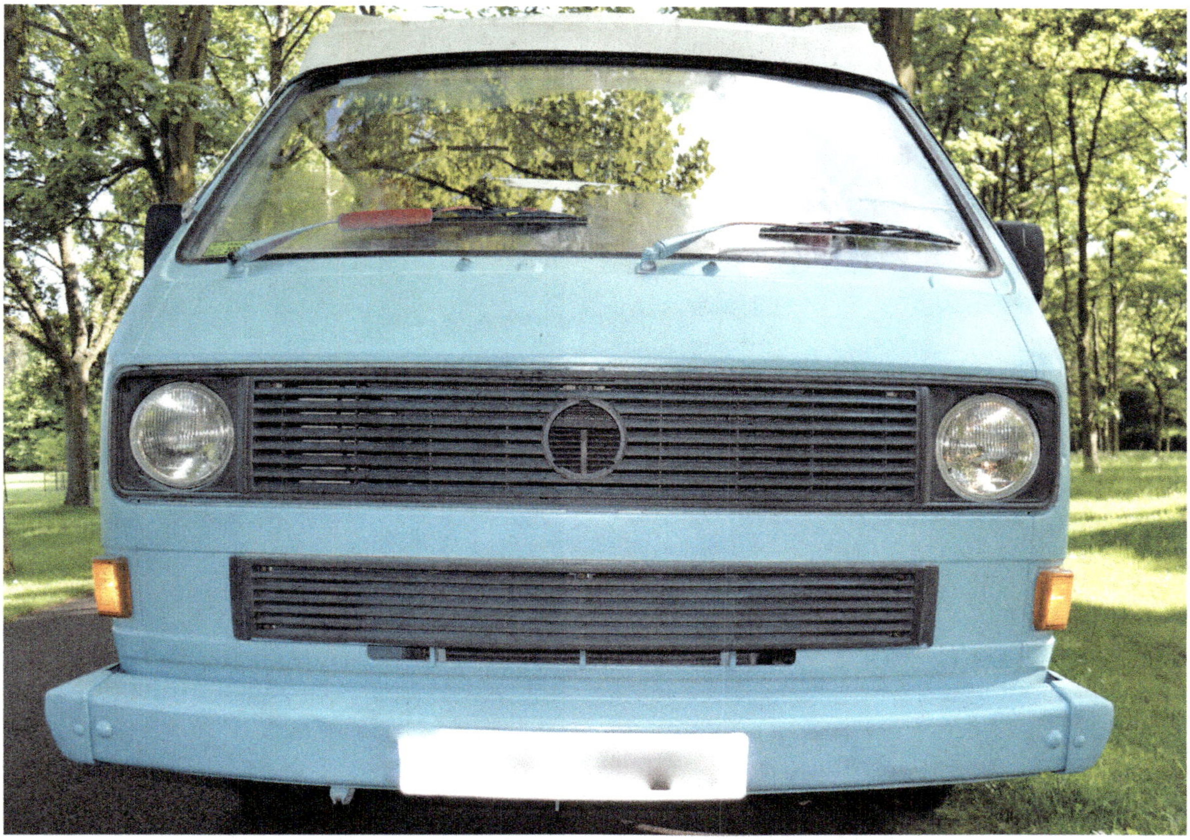

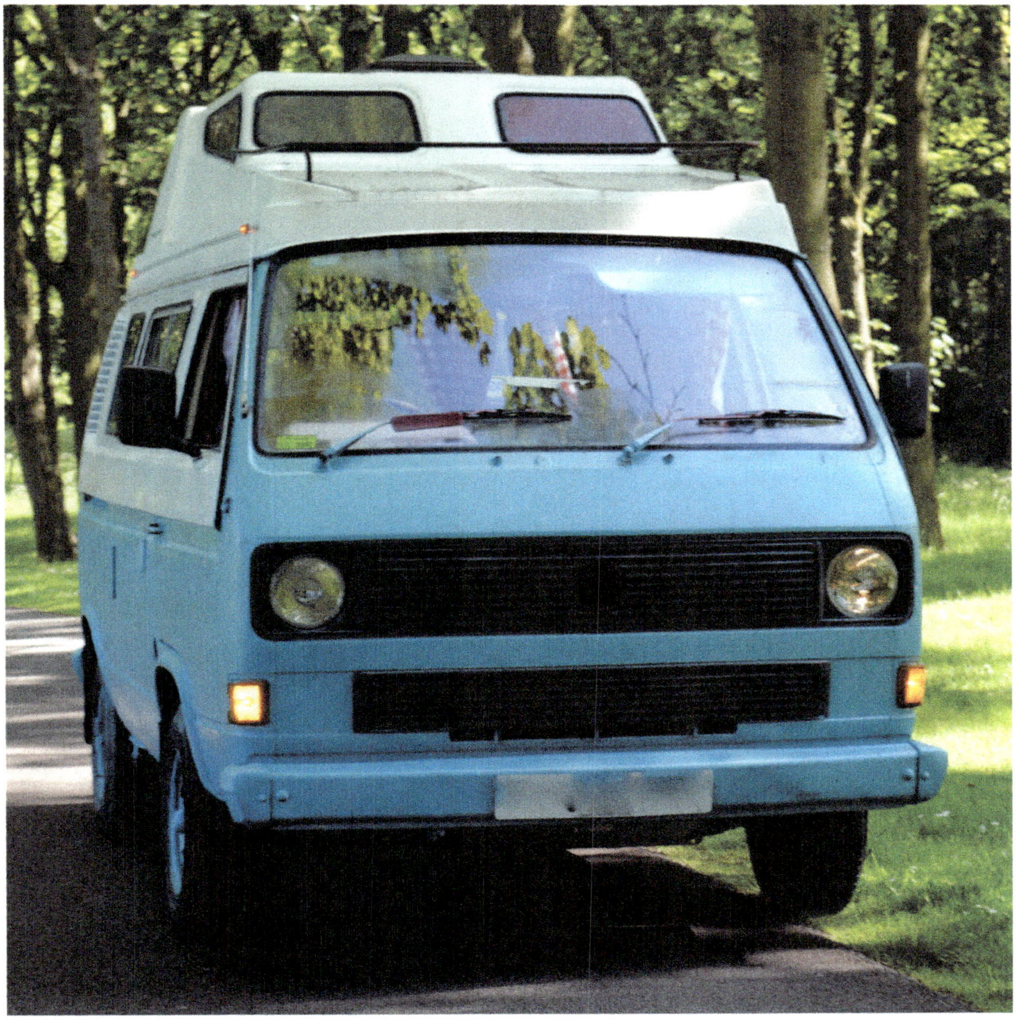

64

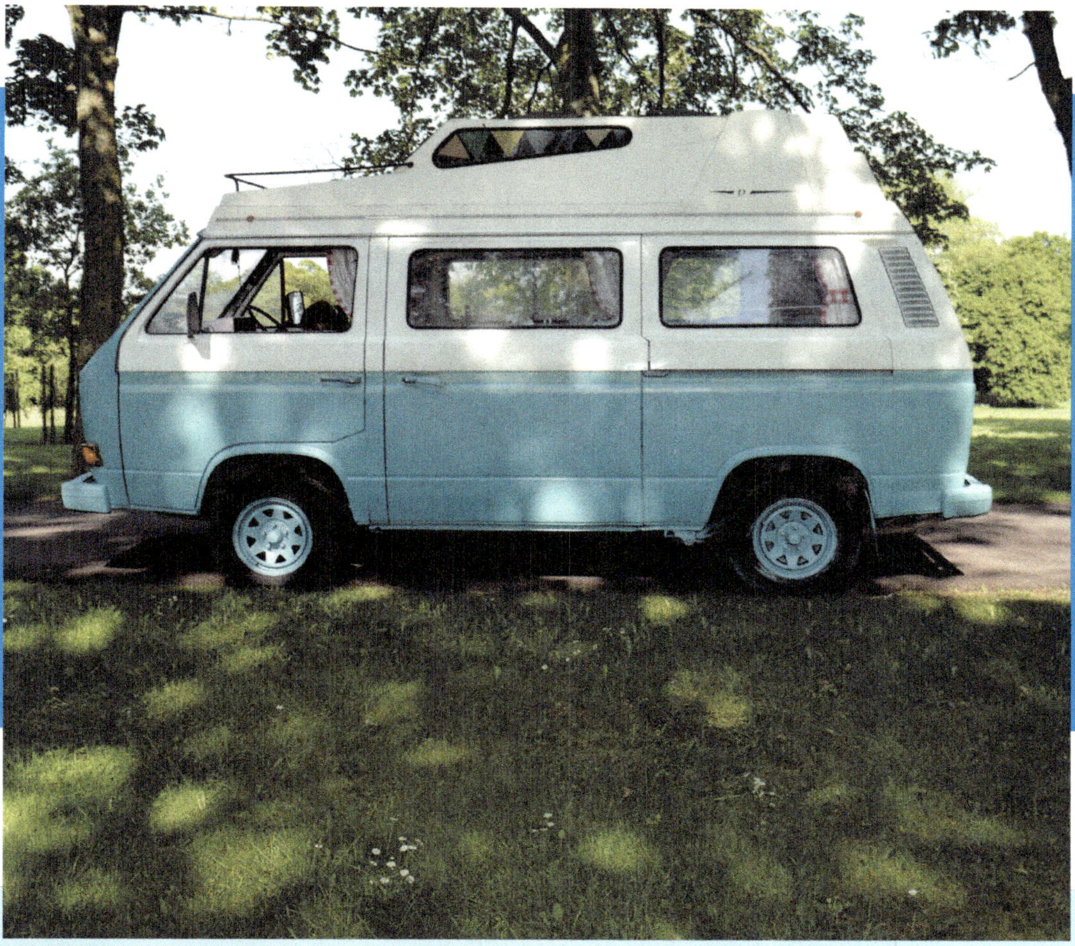

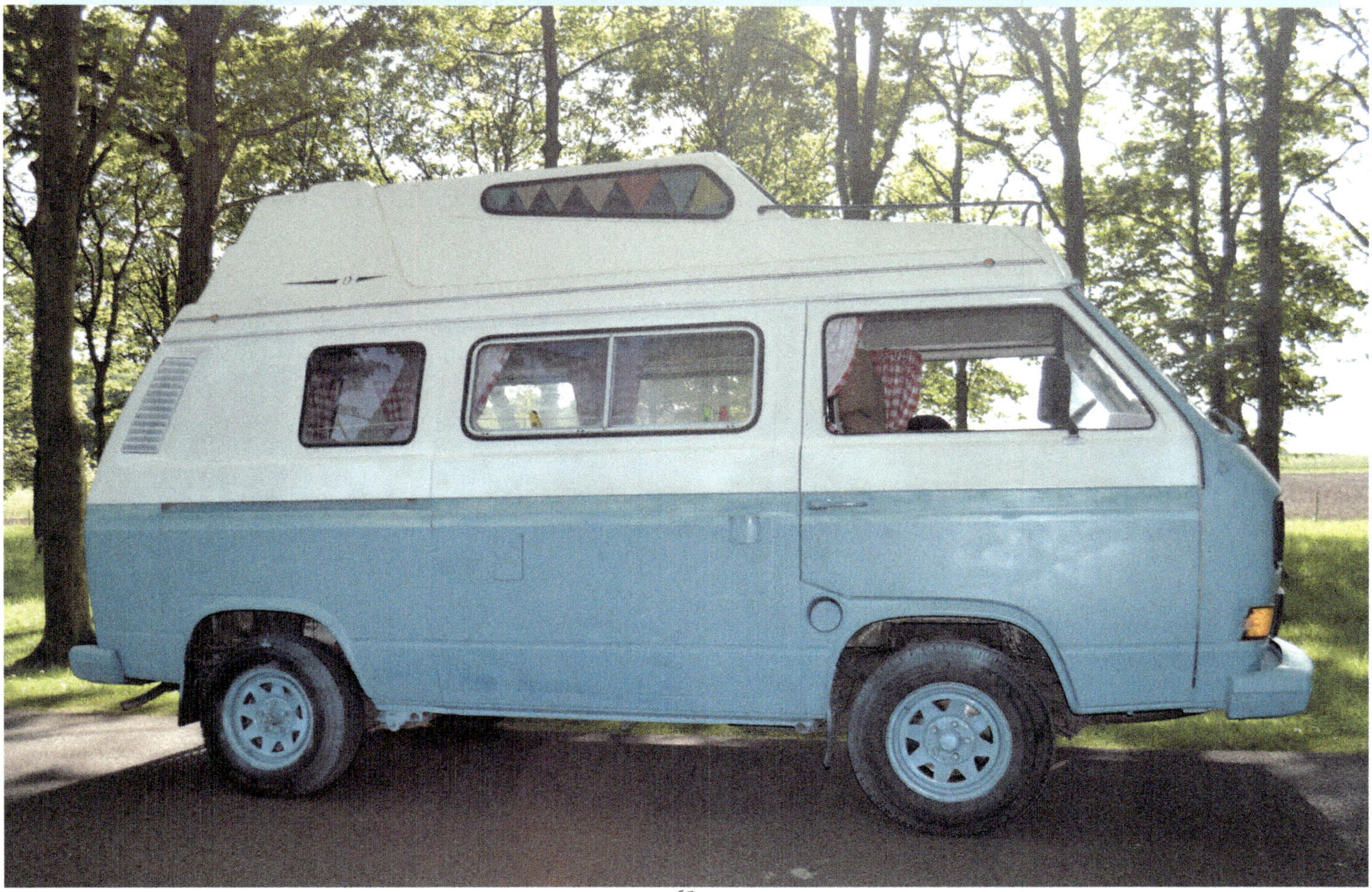

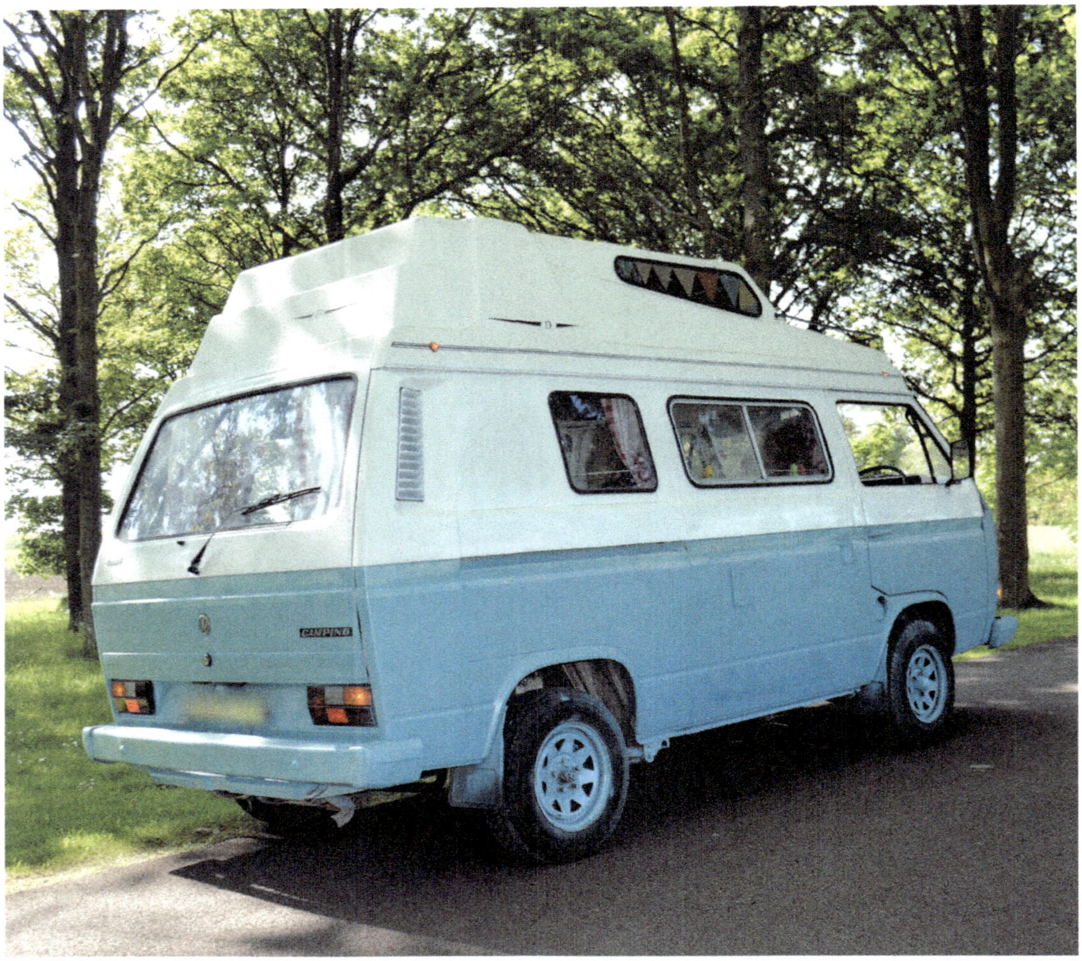

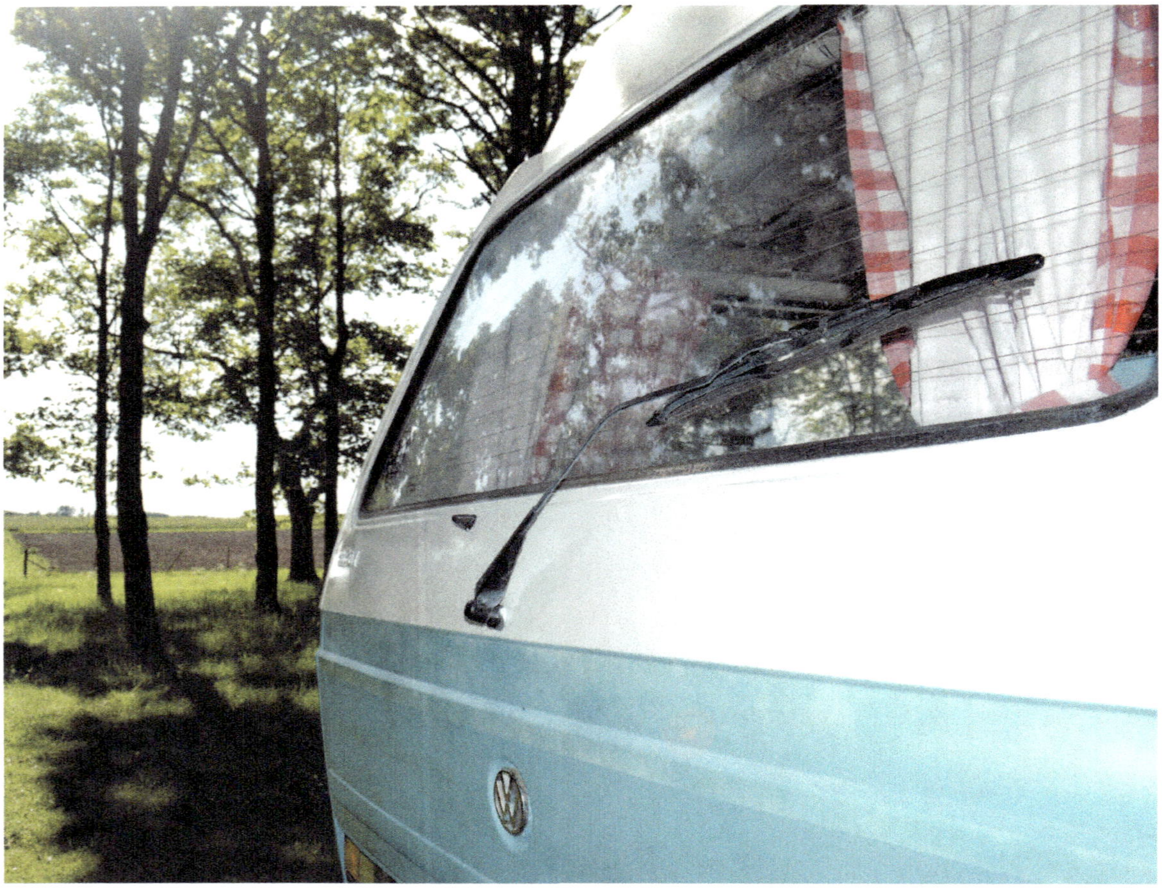

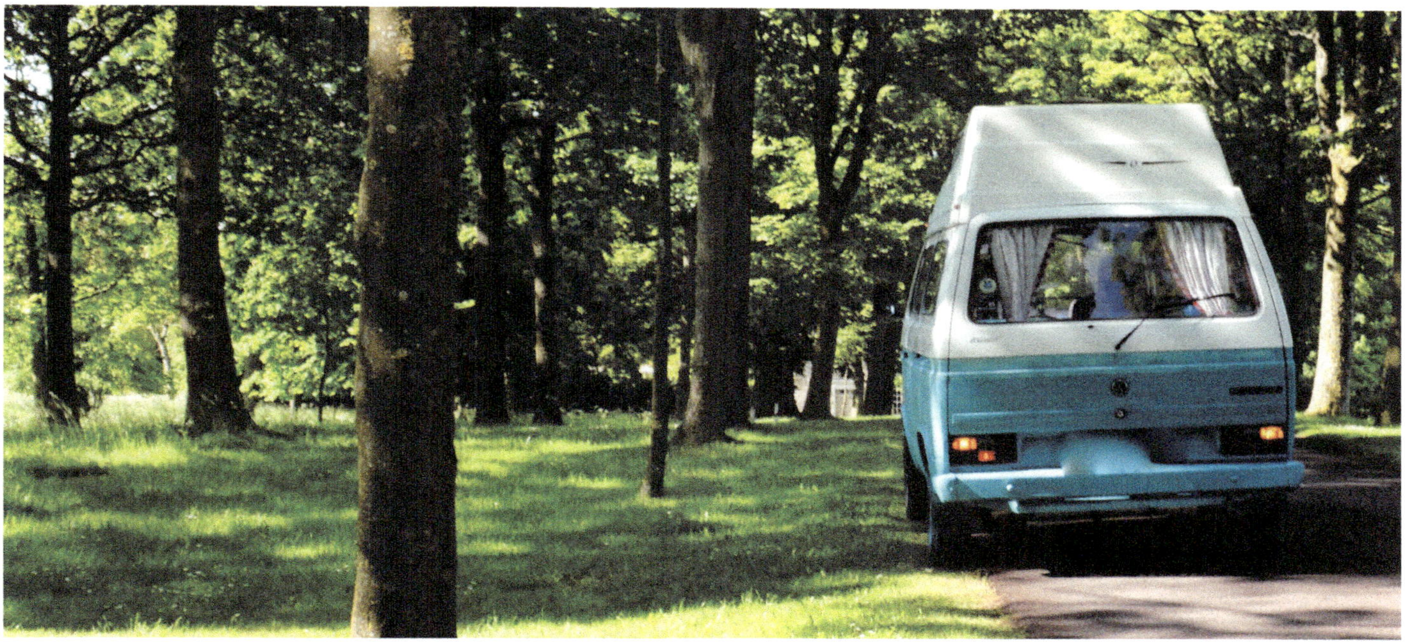

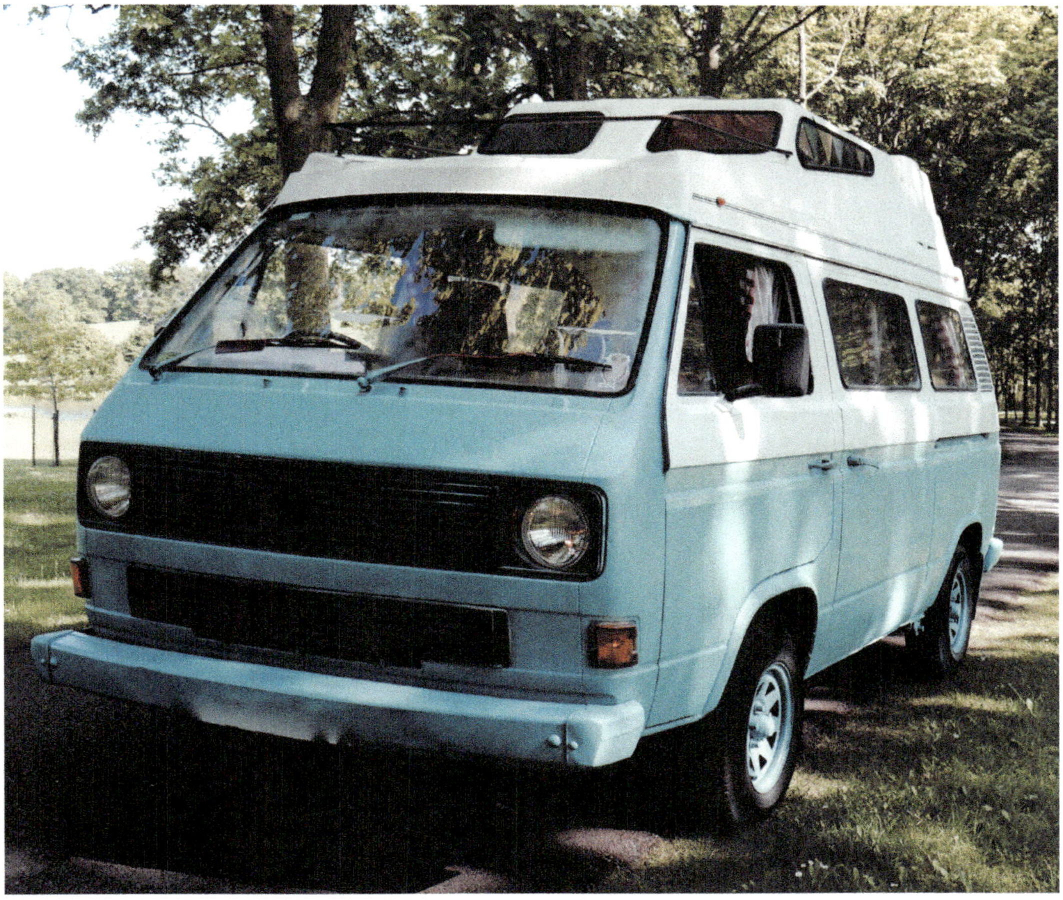

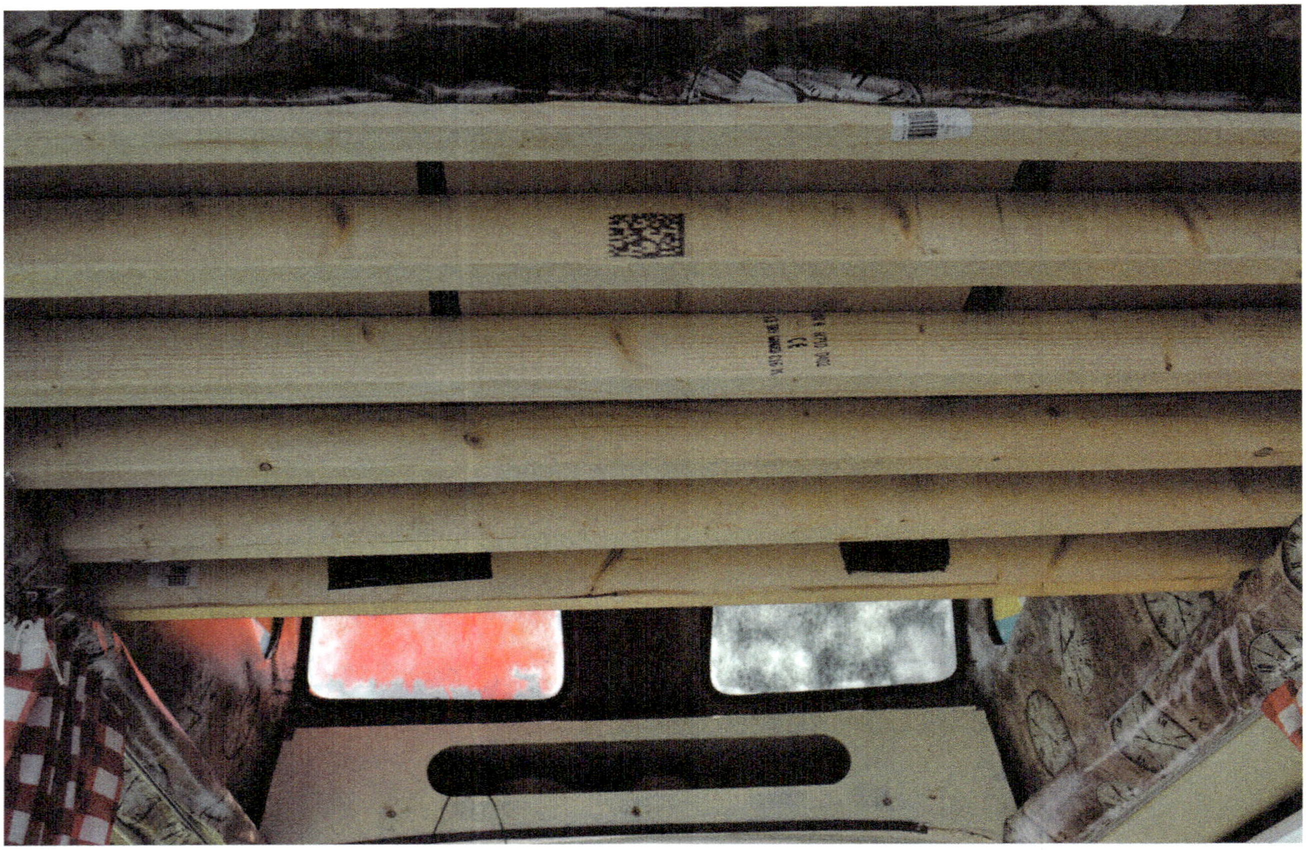

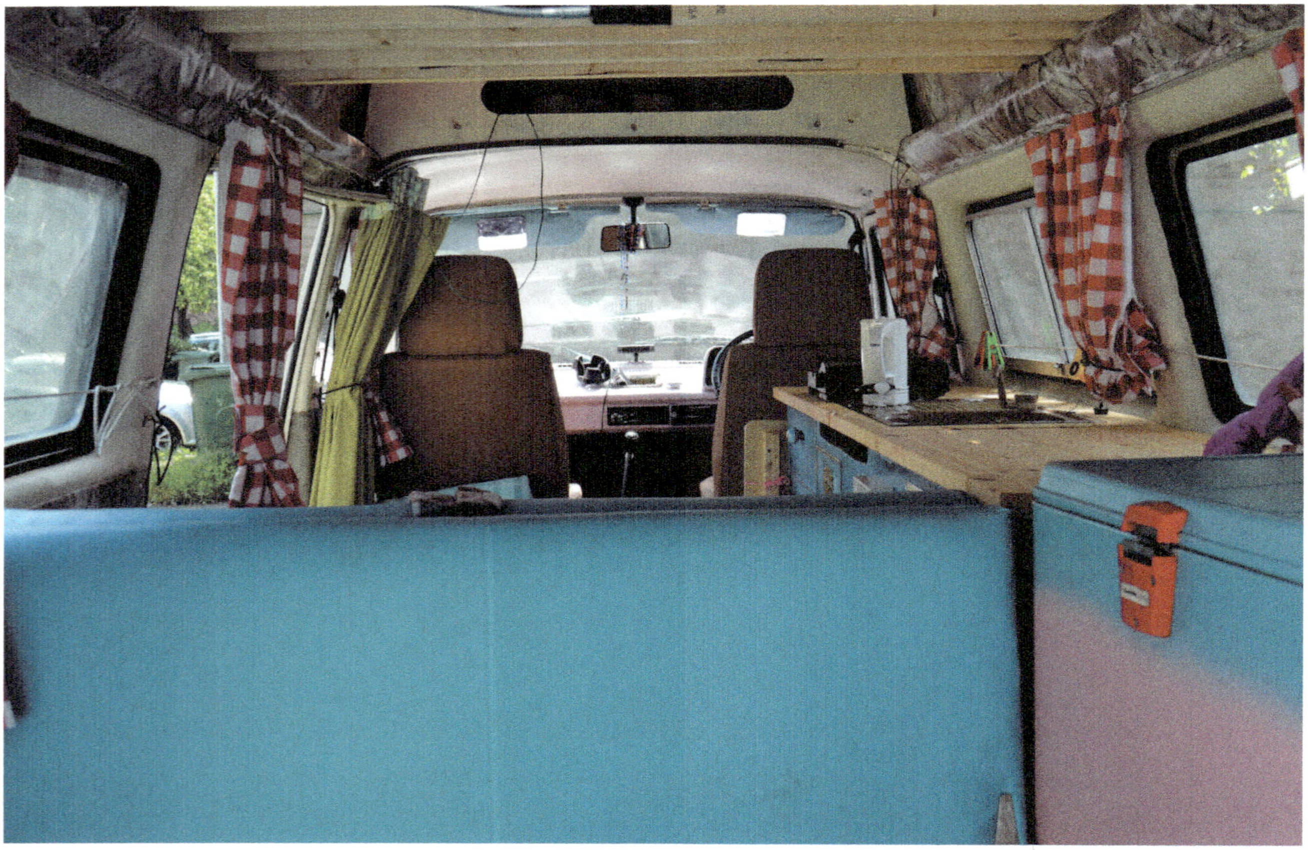

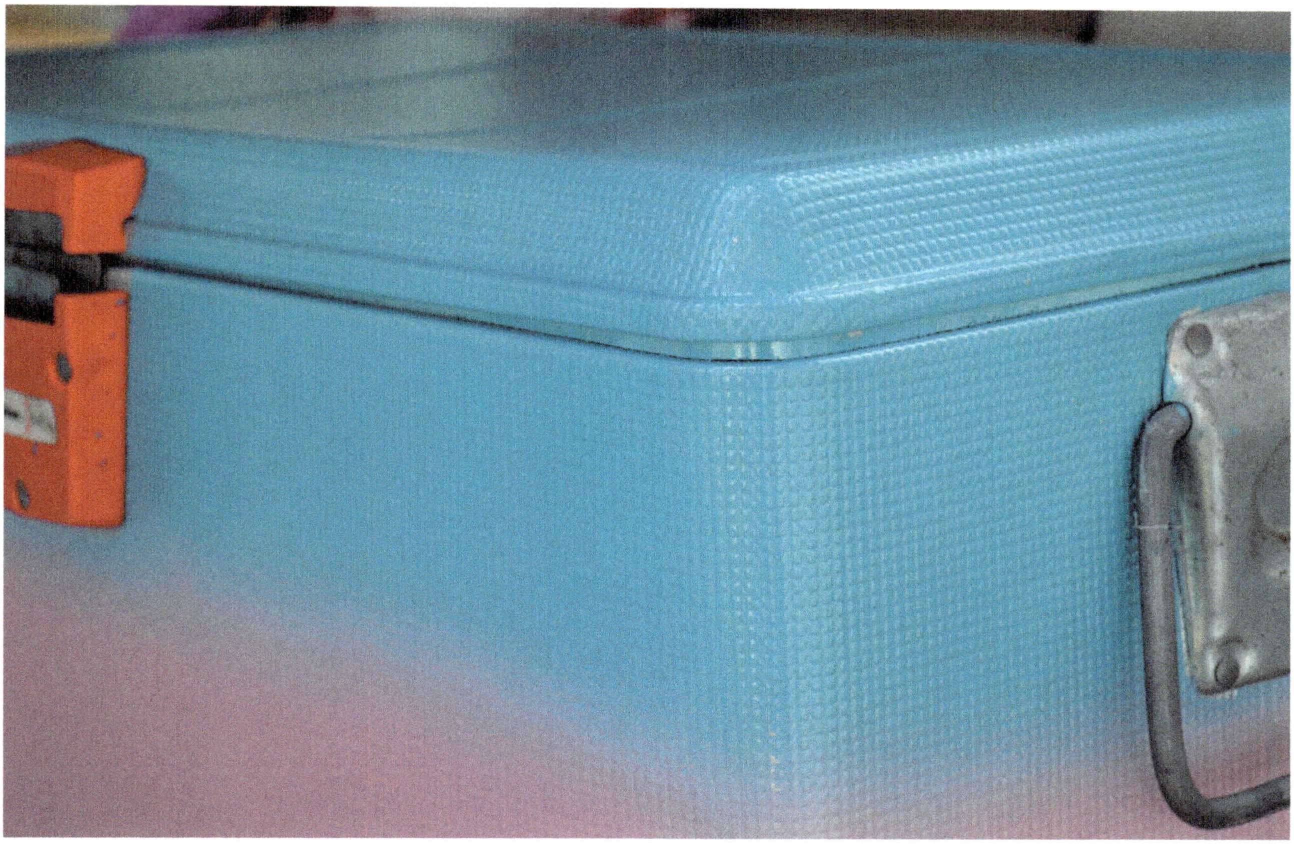

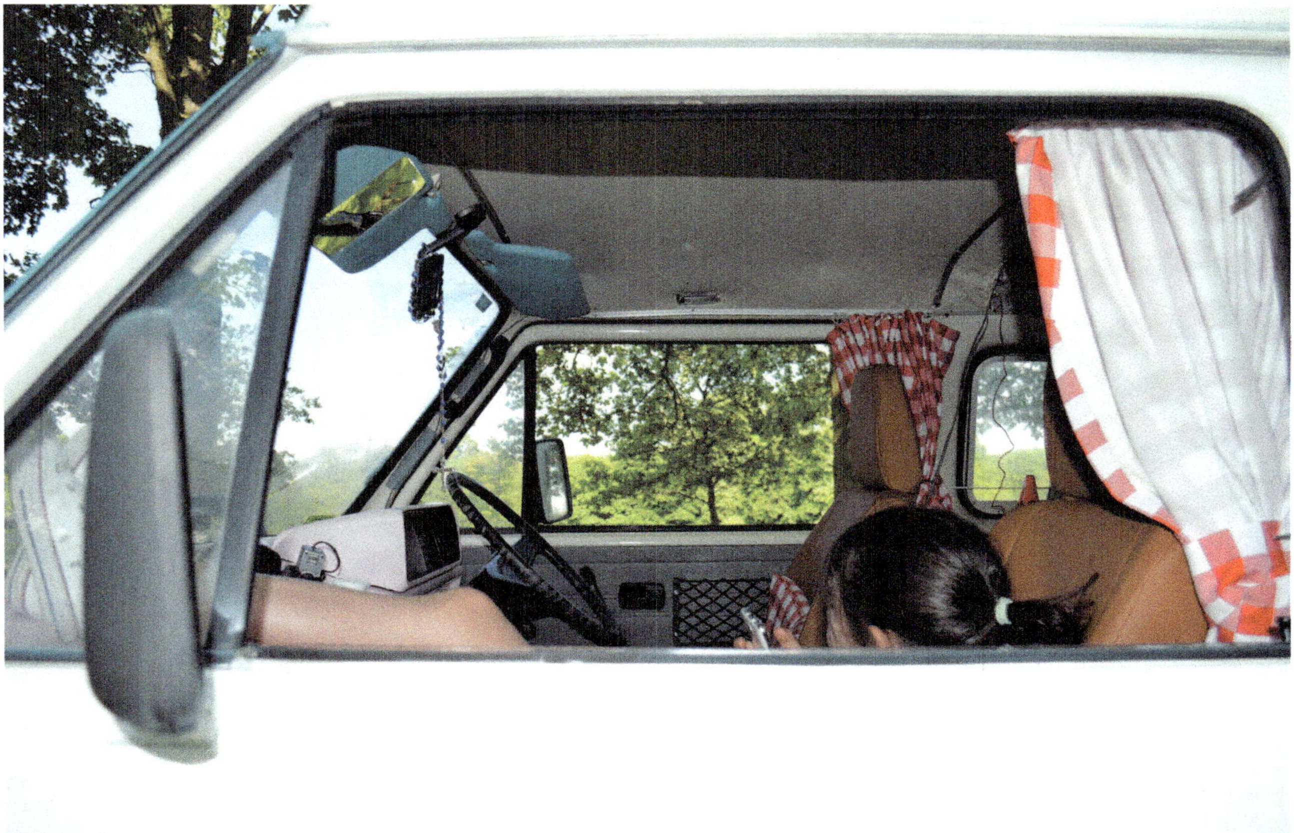

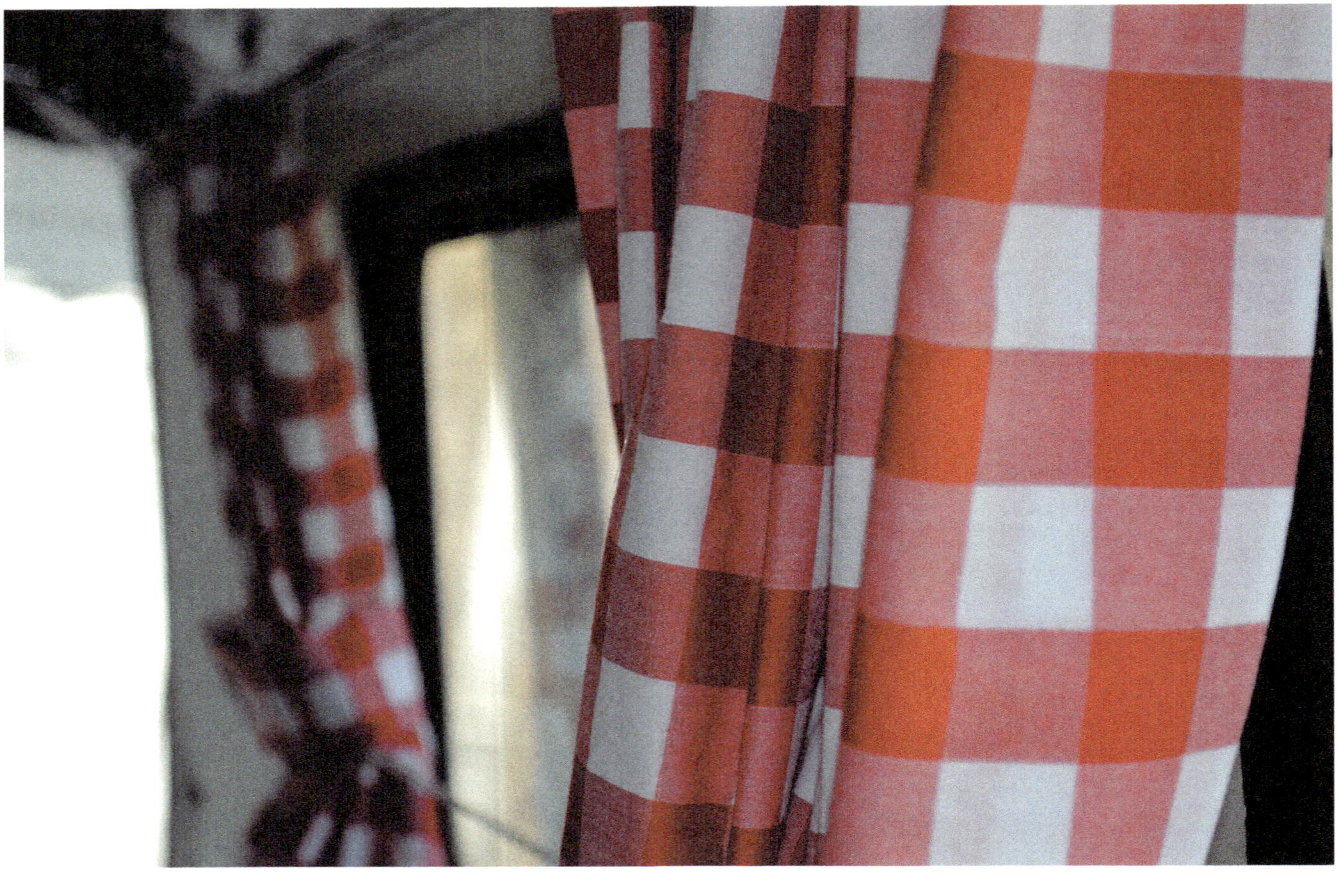

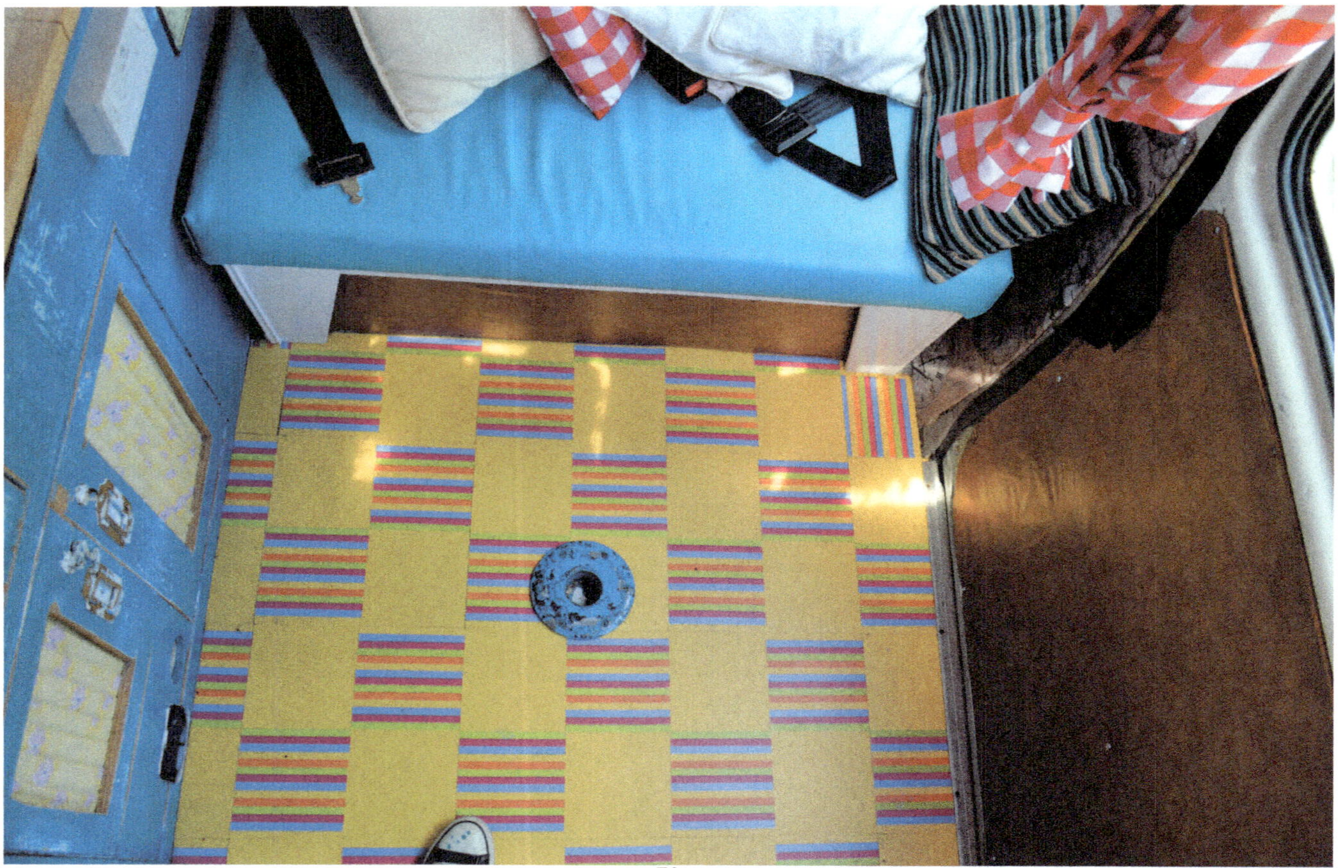

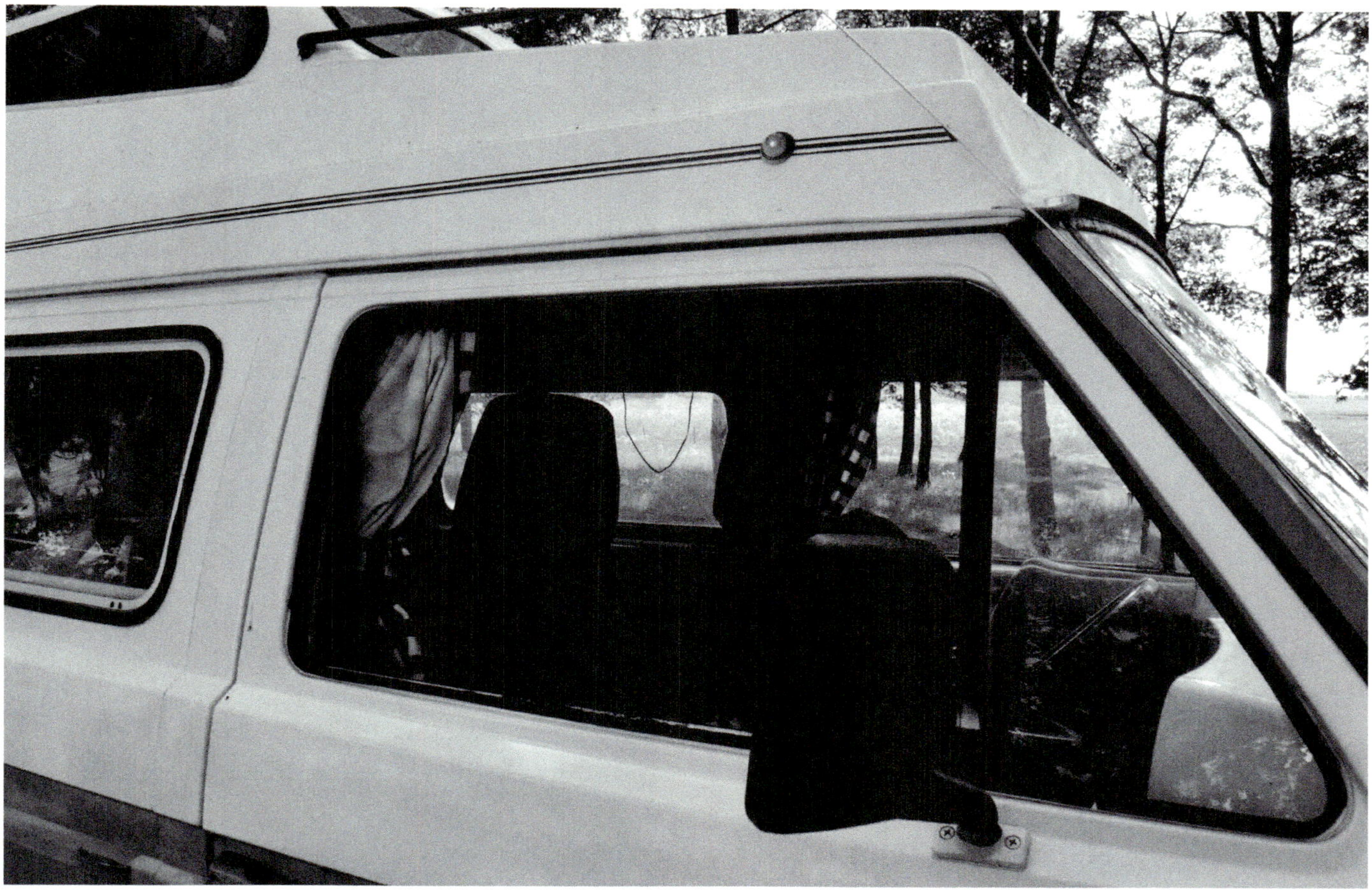

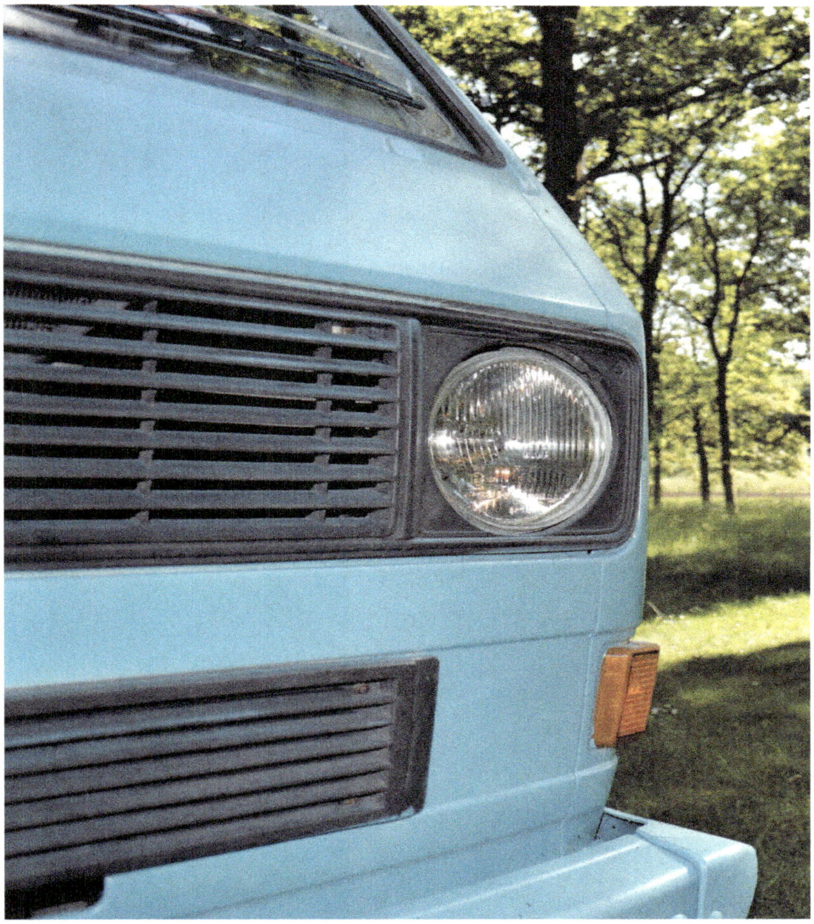

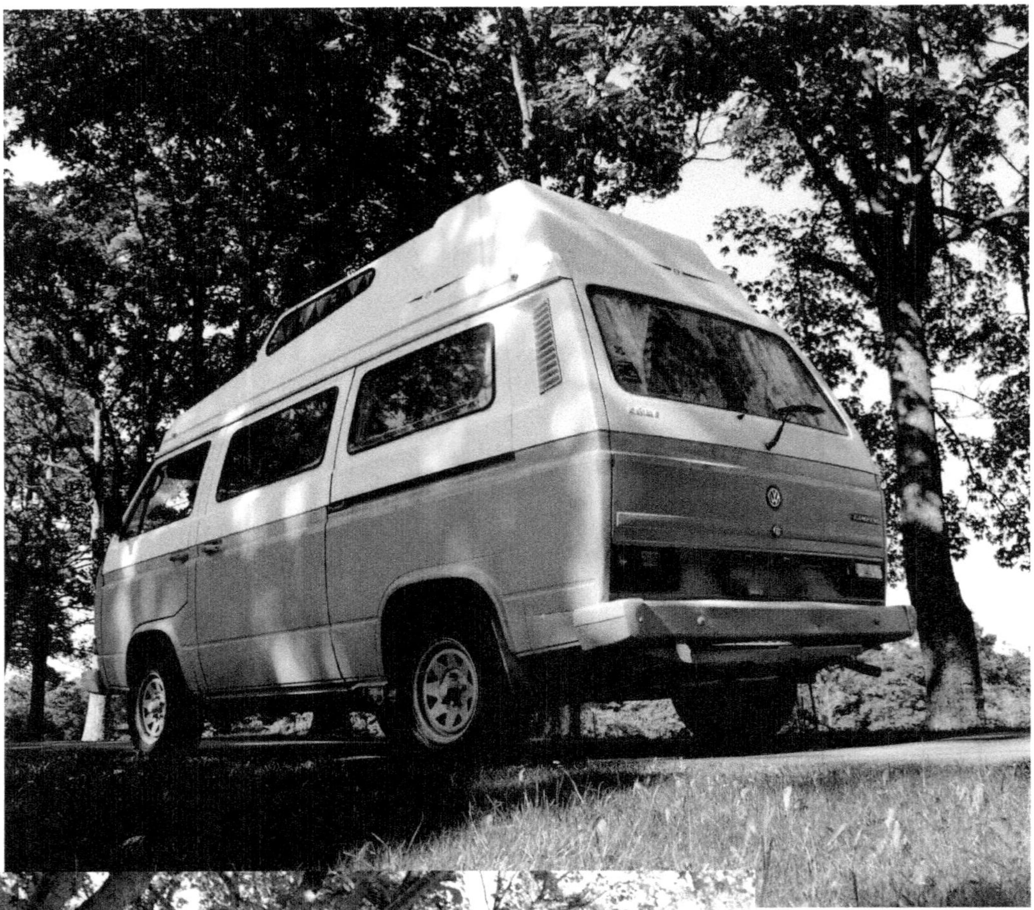

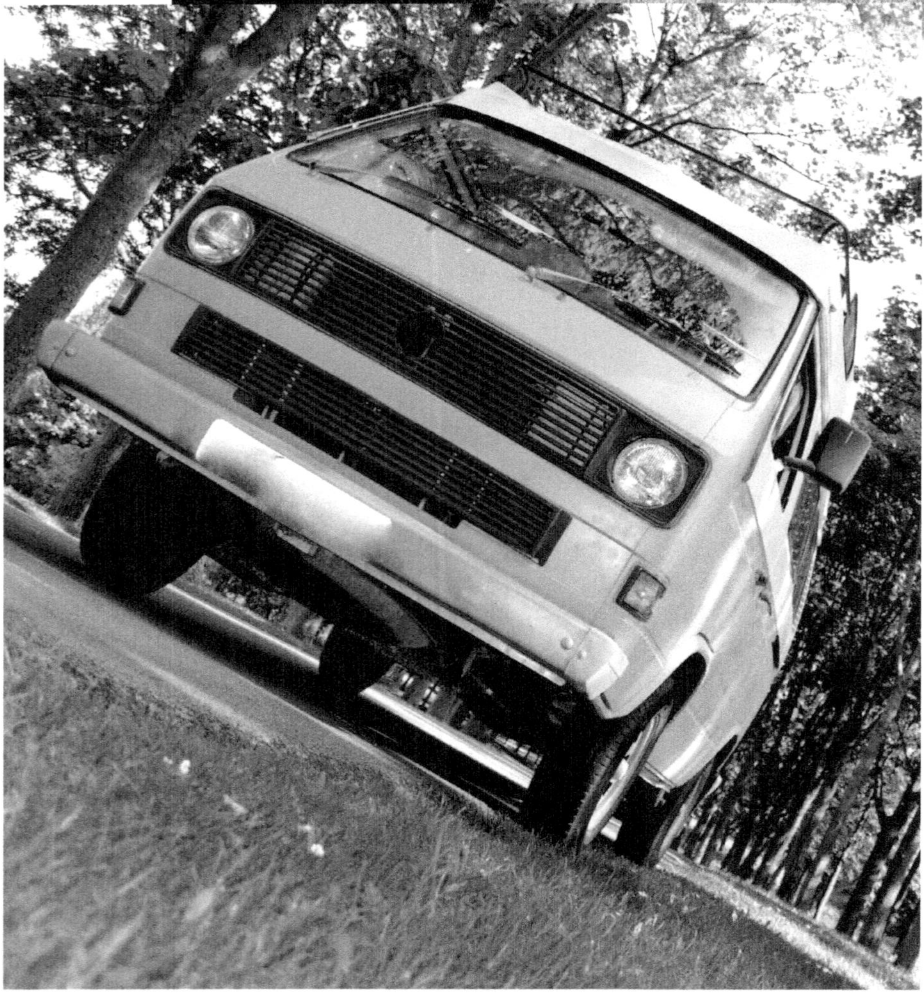

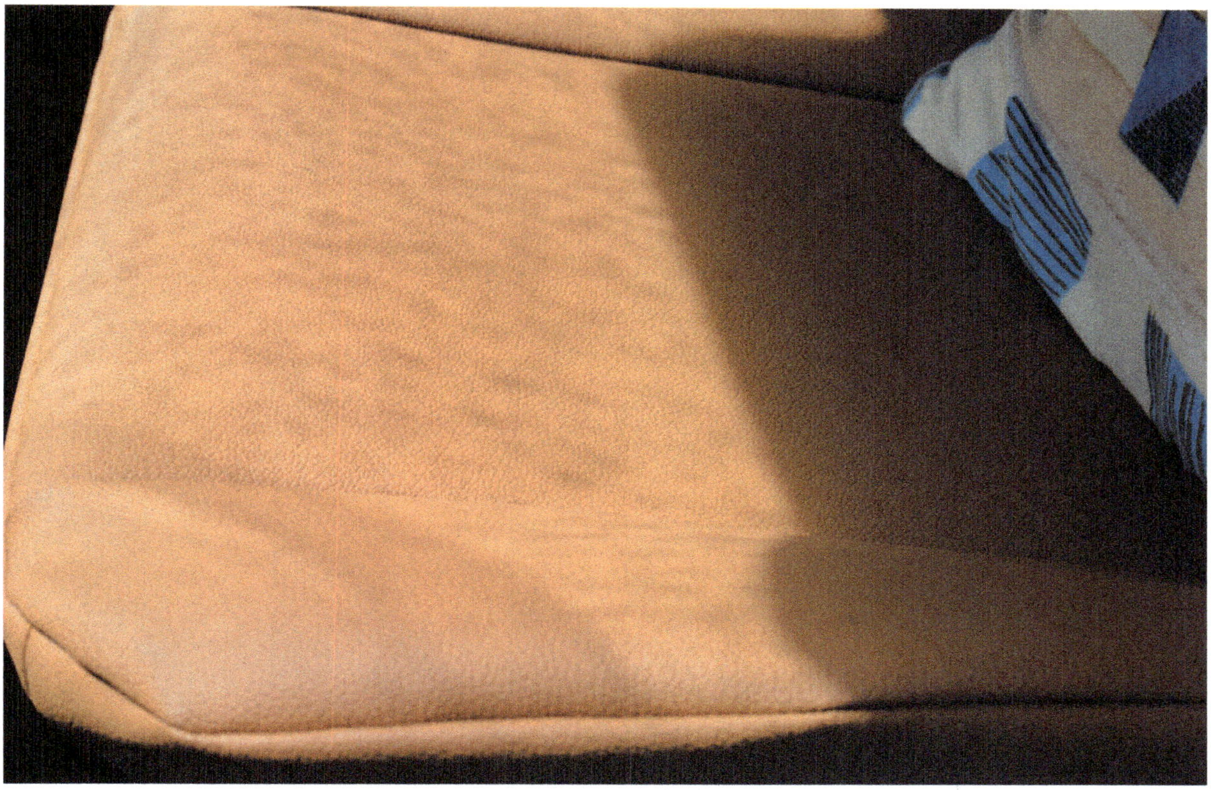

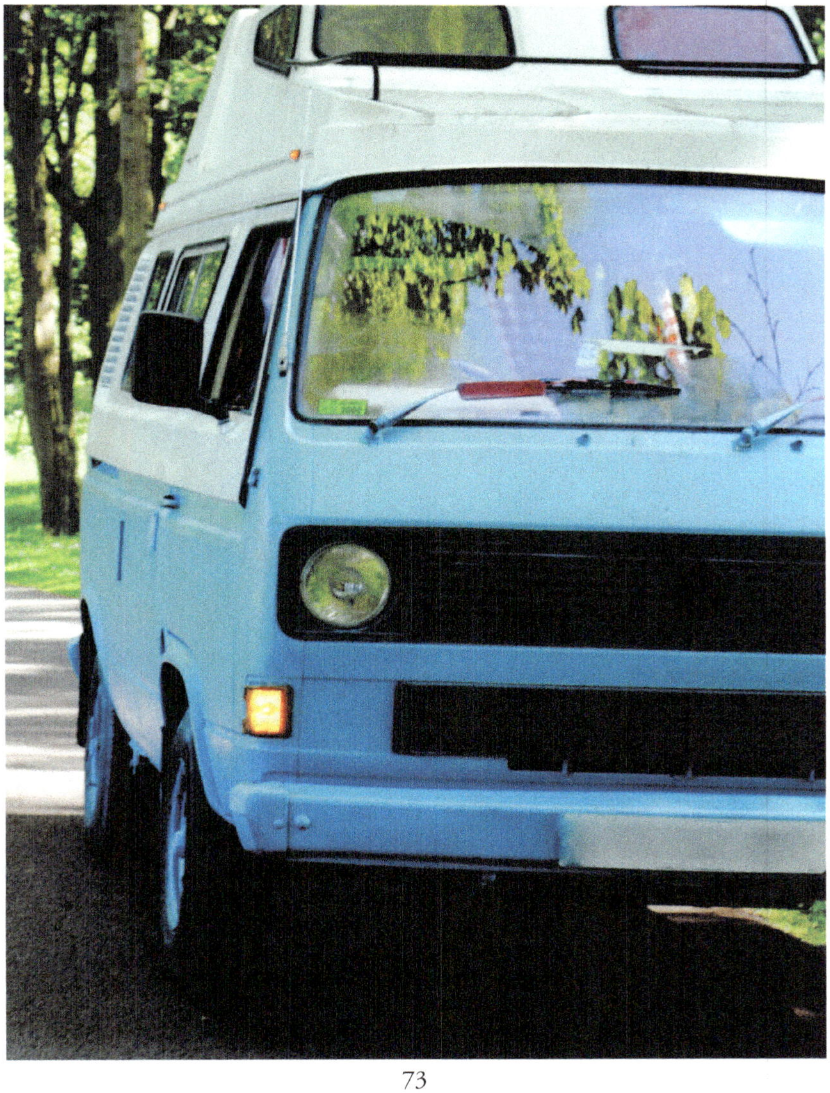

74

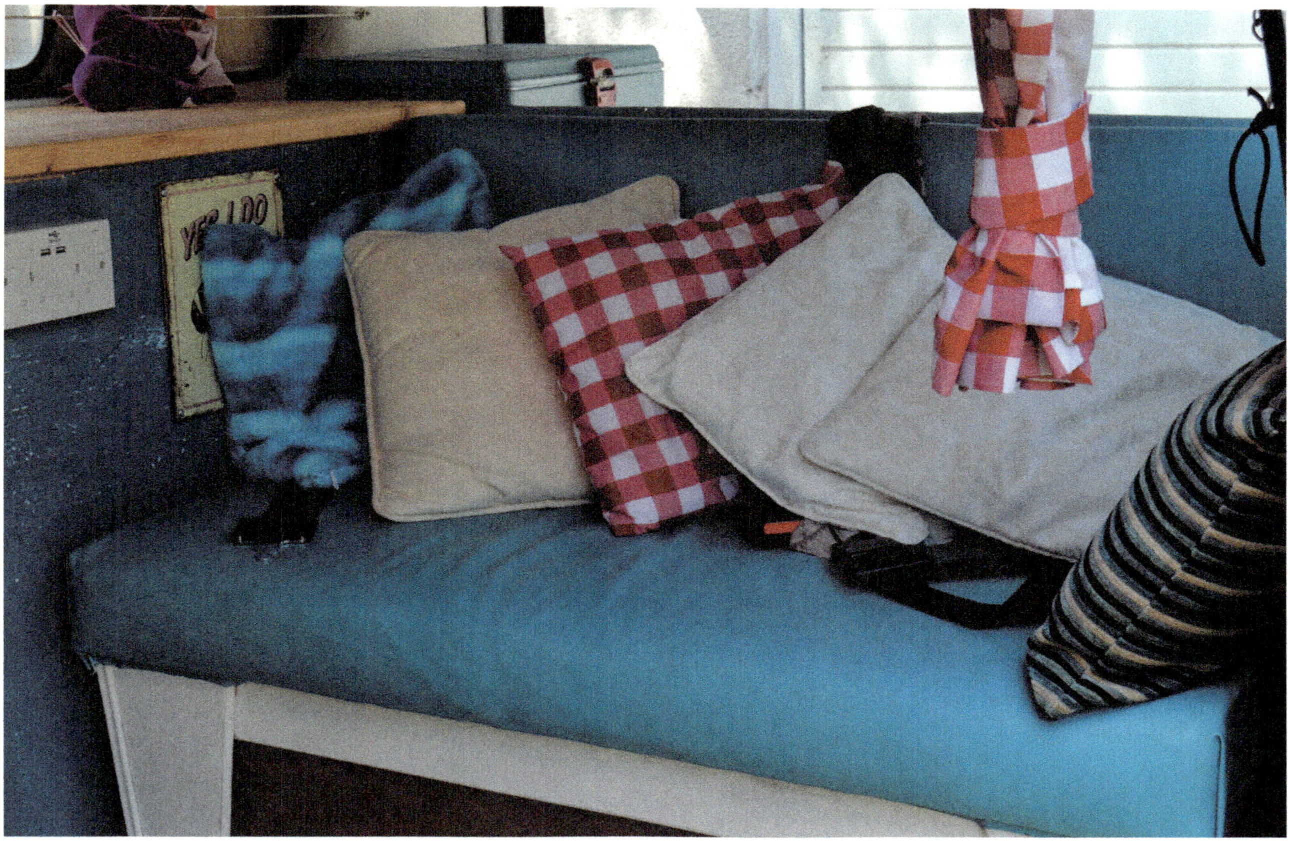

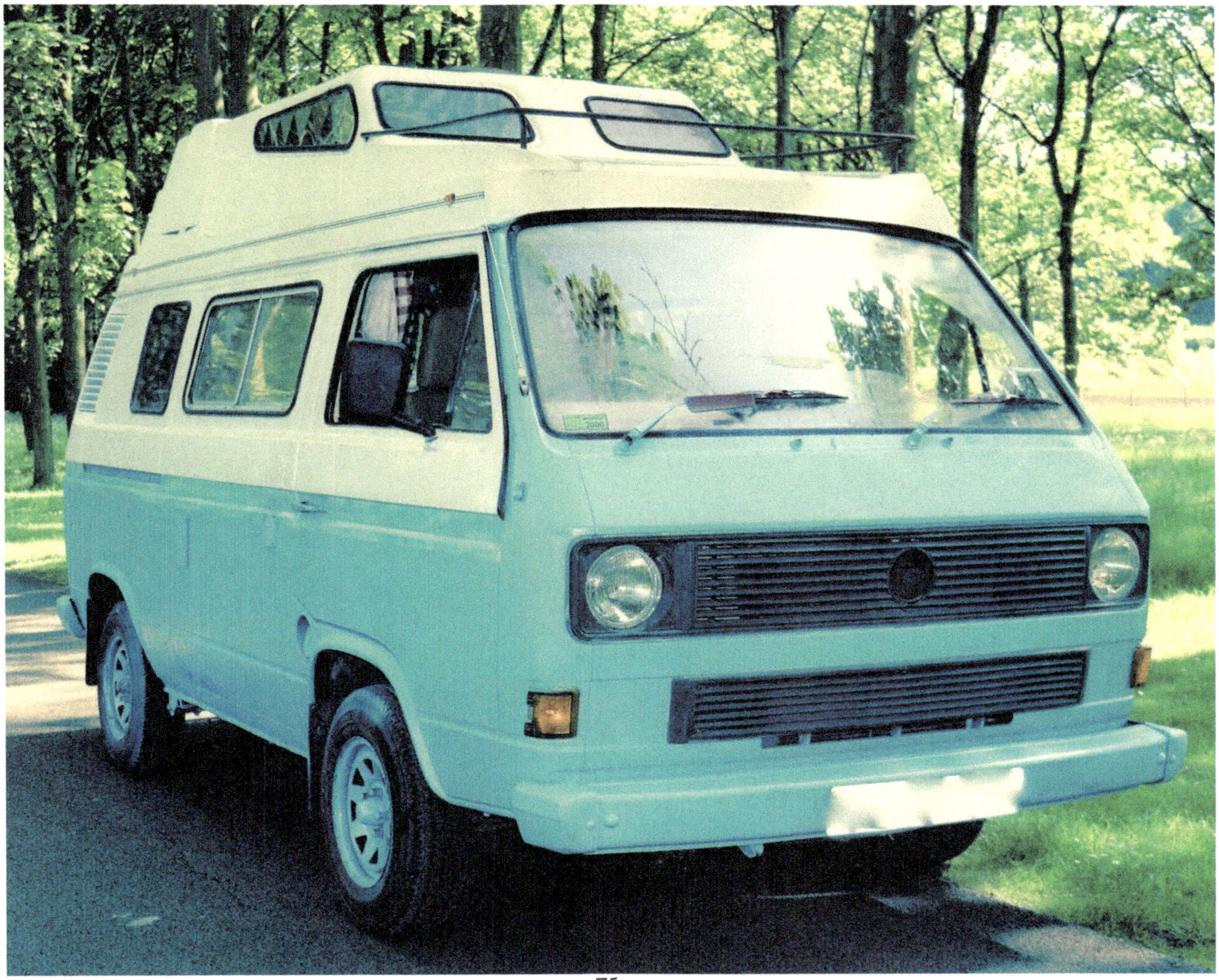

# Thank you for reading

The happy End

Lightning Source UK Ltd.
Milton Keynes UK
UKOW07f1905101017
310741UK00006B/50/P